WRITE A
REPORT

A step-by-step guide to effective report writing

John Bowden

Second Edition

How To Books

British Library cataloguing-in-publication data
A catalogue record for this book is available from the British Library.

First published in 1991 by How To Books Ltd, Plymbridge House, Estover Road, Plymouth PL6 7PZ, United Kingdom. Tel: (0752) 695745. Fax: (0752) 695699. Telex: 45635.

Reprinted 1993.
Second edition 1994.

Typeset by Concept Communications Ltd, Crayford, Kent.
Printed and bound by The Cromwell Press, Broughton Gifford, Melksham, Wiltshire.

HOW TO WRITE A REPORT

In this Series

Other titles in preparation

Contents

List of illustrations

Preface

to Second Edition

The purpose of report writing is to communicate, and effective communication is the key to success for any individual or business. Imprecise, longwinded or poorly presented reports undermine the writer's credibility and give a bad impression of his or her organisation. In contrast, clear, concise and well structured reports enhance your professional reputation and help promote a positive corporate image.

Report writing is an art, a craft — it is rarely a gift. Few people are born writers — we have to learn to do it well. The good news is that you *can* learn, and it's *never* too late. This book shows you how you can turn a routine chore into a career opportunity. It takes you step-by-step all the way from being asked to write a report through to issuing a tailor-made product which meets the needs of all your readers. It tells you how to write reports which will be:

- read without unnecessary delay;

- understood without undue effort;

- accepted and, where appropriate, acted upon.

To achieve these aims you must do more than present all the relevant facts accurately; you must communicate in a way that is both acceptable and intelligible to your readers.

The first three chapters describe the **systematic approach** needed to produce an effective report, regardless of the subject matter. Chapters 4 to 9 provide a wealth of **practical tips** that will help you get your message across. What we shall be talking about here is the **creative** side of report writing. Chapter 10 describes some common types of report in more detail.

This book will help you develop a simple, effective, yet individual report writing style. Your reports will become readily understandable, easily digestible and truly memorable. Soon you will be producing documents that people actually *want* to read. Your reputation will grow, and you will begin to exert real influence on your readers.

John Bowden

1
Preparation and Planning

The importance of careful preparation and planning cannot be stressed too highly. Trying to write a report without preparation and planning is like jumping into a car dressed only in your nightwear and driving off without knowing where you are going.

This chapter considers six questions which you should ask yourself before going any further:

1. What is the precise purpose of the report?

2. What overall objective(s) do I have?

3. Who will read the report?

4. What resources are at my disposal?

5. What information will I need to obtain?

6. How shall I present my findings?

The answers to these key questions will strongly influence the content, presentation and layout of your report. Let's take a look at them.

WHAT IS THE PRECISE PURPOSE OF THE REPORT?

If someone has asked you to prepare the report, make sure you know *precisely* what is expected of you. In other words, ask for **terms of reference.** If the response to your question is in any way ambiguous (for example, 'Just do a report on absenteeism'), it is a good idea to write down what you believe are the intended terms of reference – preferably in just one sentence – and then seek confirmation that this is indeed what is required. (For example, 'Absenteeism in the Cardiff and Edinburgh Branches of ABC Limited, 1990-1994'). It is equally important to define your precise purpose when you have initiated the report yourself. Only by continually thinking about this purpose can you expect to remain relevant throughout.

WHAT OVERALL OBJECTIVE(S) DO I HAVE?

Once you are sure of your terms of reference, ask yourself, in broad terms, what the report will seek to achieve. What **results** are you hoping for? Only when you have identified this 'bottom line' can you begin to concentrate on getting your message across effectively.

Here are some possible overall objectives for a report writer – although in practice any report is likely to be produced for some combination of these reasons:

- to inform

- to describe

- to explain

- to instruct

- to evaluate (and recommend)

- to provoke debate

- to persuade

The information you will include in your report, and the way you might arrange it will be dictated largely by your overall objective(s). For this reason the more closely you identify your objective(s), the more useful your report is likely to be.

WHO WILL READ THE REPORT?

Identify and assess your readership
This is your next step, to try to find out something about them. You could ask yourself:

- Are they alike or mixed?

- Are they used to reading and understanding reports?

- How much time will they spend on this report?

- Are they familiar with the subject?

- What do they already know?

- What else will they need to know?

- What are their attitudes to the subject and to me?

- Are they likely to be sympathetic to my objective(s)?

- What is the relationship between them and me?

You would write different things, and in different ways, when addressing your boss, your staff or members of the public.

Meet your readers
If possible, find answers to questions such as:

- Do they use, or at least understand technical terms?

- What sort of publications are in their offices?

If you cannot meet them in person, then phone them or ask someone about them. Failing this, at least establish their occupations. This will give you some useful clues, from which you might ask:

- What deductions can I make about their education, training and technical ability?

- What priorities, attitudes and prejudices are they likely to have?

Obviously you are generalising; accountants are not all alike, nor are publicans, or any other group. However, you can make some reasonable assumptions about them, which gives you something to work on.

Being appropriate

Always remember that you will be writing for real people. Good doctors talk to fellow professionals in a very different way from how they talk to patients, in terms of both content and presentation. Similarly, try to write in the way that is most appropriate for your readers.

Clearly, the more diverse your readership, the more difficult it is to pitch the report at the right level. Is one reader more important than the others? If so, aim the report at him or her. If not, there are ways of getting around the problem of a mixed readership. It can be done by issuing two or more reports or – and this is more likely – by including a summary, a glossary, and/or some appendixes. In this way the interests of a wide range of readers can be accommodated.

WHAT RESOURCES ARE AT MY DISPOSAL?

You need to know what resources will be available to you before, during, and after your project, such as:

- How many working hours have been allocated to it?

- What is my budget?

- What equipment or apparatus will be at my disposal?

- When will it be available?

Until you know your resources (or possibly your lack of resources) you cannot realistically decide what information you will gather or how you will present your findings.

At this planning stage you should also reserve a quiet and peaceful room where you can write the report once the project has been completed.

WHAT INFORMATION WILL I NEED TO OBTAIN?

Your answer to this question will depend on your answers to the previous four questions. In other words, it will be determined by:

- your precise purpose,
- your overall objective(s),
- your readers' needs, and
- your resources.

Your aim is make the best use of your limited resources in order to obtain **adequate relevant information** which, when properly handled and presented, will satisfy the first three of these requirements.

Analyse the subject to **determine the main features** to be examined. Many report writers use patterned notes to help identify the information they will need (see Chapter 2, 'How should I record my findings?'). It is often useful to make use of the **Pareto Principle** which states that 80 per cent of what is important is represented by 20 per cent of what exists (for example, 80 per cent of a company's revenue may be generated by 20 per cent of its customers). Concentrate on this 20 per cent.

HOW SHALL I PRESENT MY FINDINGS?

You are now in a position to think about the overall plan of your report. This is known as the **skeletal framework**. It is like drawing up the plans for a new house. Not only will it show its overall structure, it will also remind you of the materials (information) you will need to gather before the process of construction can begin. A well-planned skeletal framework is the **key** to effective report writing since it enables the writer:

- to be sure there is no misunderstanding over the terms of reference,
- to have an overview of the entire report,
- to be reminded of what information must be collected, and what is not needed,
- to order his or her thoughts before considering how they should be expressed,
- to appreciate the significance of and the relationship between the various items of information that will be gathered, and
- to maintain a sense of perspective while gathering this information and, later, when writing the report.

You may find it necessary or desirable to revise this framework once the project has been completed; for example, you might need to highlight some particularly important finding. However, it is far easier to revise a skeletal framework than to attempt to structure your findings without an initial plan.

The skeletal framework you choose will be influenced by these factors:

- the requirements of the person who commissioned the report

- house-style

- custom and conventions

- your objective(s)

- your readership

- common sense

Let's consider each factor in turn.

The requirements of the person who commissioned the report
If possible, agree the framework of the report with the person who asked you to produce it. In this way he or she will be *expecting* a structure similar to the one you will be providing. After weeks or perhaps months of hard work, it is extremely frustrating to hear those dreaded words: 'But I expected you to present it entirely differently from that'.

House-style
Many organisations have their own house-style. For example, do they talk about house-style, house style, house-rules or house rules? Such consistency helps the writer, the reader, and the typist or printer. It also projects the same organisational image to the outside world. Sensible house-style will help the writer by providing practical guidance. However, it should never be so rigid as to impede individual style.

Custom and convention
Some routine reports are always presented in the same way, often

on standard forms. For example, they may compare certain key statistics from one period to another. If you are asked to complete such a report, you will have little or no scope to influence its presentation. Simply refer to previous reports to see what is required. However, if you believe that the existing format could be improved in some way – and if you can justify this – then do not be afraid to say so.

Your objective(s) and your readership

You now know that it helps to establish your objective. Perhaps you intend to persuade your chairperson (your reader) to authorise the purchase of product A rather than product B (your objective). Or perhaps you wish to instruct your staff (your readers) how to use a particular item of machinery (your objective). Clearly, these are different messages to different audiences, and what you say and how you say it will be strongly influenced by these two factors. The best single piece of advice to bear in mind is never *write* anything that you would not *say* to your readers face-to-face. You will find some suggested skeletal frameworks suitable for many common types of report in Chapter 10.

Common sense

Remember that the task of the report writer is to supply his or her readers with the information they need in a form they can understand. A report is a means to an end – to inform, to explain, and so on – it is *not* an end in itself. Your aim therefore is to communicate effectively, not to produce a literary masterpiece.

Attracting the reader

The report will succeed only if it is read without unnecessary delay, it is understood without undue effort, its findings are accepted and, where appropriate, acted upon. You are writing for real people so design a framework that *they* will find attractive and useful.

Where practicable, talk to your future readers; there is little worse than attempting to produce a report in a vacuum. What kind of structure would they like to see? Do not promise to meet their every demand, but let them know that their views are important and appreciated (which they should be). If you are able to produce a report which goes a long way to meeting its readers' express needs, you will have gone a long way towards getting the results you are hoping for. Any reader who feels that a report has been prepared with him or her in mind is unlikely to reject its findings.

Planning a structure

Think very carefully about the structure of your report. The time and thought that you spend on it at this stage will make a vast difference to the effectiveness of the work that will follow. It will also greatly enhance the appearance and the professionalism of the report.

What options are available to you? An effective report will have three broad sections – a beginning, a middle and an end. It is your task to select the most suitable components to build up each of these sections. All reports have a number of commonly recognised components including:

The beginning

- Title page
- Foreword
- Preface
- Acknowledgements
- Contents page
- Summary or Abstract
- Introduction

The middle

- Main body, including substructures

The end

- Conclusions
- Recommendations
- Appendixes
- References
- Bibliography
- Glossary
- Index

Do not be concerned about the large number of components that may be used; no report ever uses all of them. However, it is as well to know something about each of these components for two reasons:

— You can then choose the ones best suited to your report, and
— You may be asked to include one or more of them.

Let's take a look at each of these components; this will help when
thinking about a simple framework that is suitable for many types
of report.

Title page
Every report should have a title page. This tells the reader (and any
potential reader) what the report is about. A good title page will
include the following information:

● The title

● The name and position of the person who authorised the
 report

● The name of the author(s)

● His, her or their position within the organisation

● The name of the organisation

● The date the report was issued

● A reference number

● Copyright information, if necessary

● Its degree of confidentiality

● The distribution list

The **title** should be clear, concise and relevant; restate your terms
of reference in your own words. Do not choose a title which is
similar to any other report title. Providing a **subtitle** is a good way
of keeping the title crisp while also providing more detail about its
content. Make sure the title is more prominent than any headings
that appear in the report.

Then say who **commissioned** the report (for example, 'Produced
at the request of. . .').

The decision about whether to give your first **name and any**

qualifications you may have attained should be dictated by house-style. However, as a general rule, people within your organisation will not need to be reminded of your qualifications whereas relevant qualifications will add authority to a report which is distributed externally. In the same way it is not necessary to say that you **work for** ABC Ltd, if the report is for internal circulation alone. The **date** on the report should be the date it was actually *issued*, not when it was sent to the typist or printer. Write this date in full to avoid possible ambiguities. For example, the date 12.8.95 means 12 August 1995, in Britain. In the USA it means 8 December 1995.

The **reference number** given to the report will depend on company practice. Some organisations number all reports sequentially; others do so by department and yet others add some personal reference (perhaps the initials of the author).

The decision whether to refer to **copyright** depends on the nature of the report. For the report writer the main interest in the English law of copyright is its intention to prevent the copying of a 'substantial part' of any literary work without permission. The word 'literary' covers any work expressed in printing or writing, provided it is substantial enough to have involved some literary skill and labour of composition. If you wish to know more about this, refer to the current edition of the *Writers' and Artists' Yearbook* at your local reference library.

You may decide to stamp your report '**Secret**' or '**Confidential**'. The latter is a particularly useful marking when the report is about a member of staff, as it would be a strong defence against any subsequent charge of libel. Again you may wish to refer to the current edition of the *Writers' and Artists' Yearbook* for further information. However, do not overdo it. The most routine reports arouse exceptional interest when marked 'Secret'. Conversely a report giving a foolproof method of how to win the football pools would probably go unnoticed as long as it was not given a security marking.

Finally, the title page should include the **distribution list** of the report. Ask the person who requested the report to tell you who should see it. Their names will generally be listed in order of seniority. However if you foresee any problems or disputes, perhaps because of internal politics, or if the report is to be sent outside your organisation, list the recipients alphabetically or by geographical location. Also remember to include at least one copy for file. Record this at the foot of the list.

Foreword
This component is rarely used in a report. When it is included it is generally not written by the report writer but by some (other) acknowledged expert in the field – perhaps the person who commissioned the report. A foreword should be concise.

Preface
This is another uncommon component. It is used when a writer wishes to convey some personal background details behind the report's production.

Acknowledgements
This section is used to convey your thanks to people and/or organisations who helped during the preparation of the report. For example they may have provided information, help, finance, or granted permission for you to use some copyright material. Do not go over the top with your thanks and try to keep it balanced and in perspective. For example, you may 'wish to record (your) thanks to Mr X' (who assisted you for an hour) and later 'to convey (your) special thanks to Mrs Y' (who helped for a week). If a large number of people assisted you it may not be possible, or even desirable, to name them all. One way of getting round this is 'to thank the management and staff of ABC Ltd'. Alternatively, you could record a blanket acknowledgement such as: 'I also wish to thank everyone else who assisted during the preparation of this report'. In this way you are covered if you have forgotten to mention somebody by name. As a general rule it is unnecessary to express your gratitude to people who would have been expected to help you (such as your staff or members of the typing pool), unless they made some special effort on your behalf. Read acknowledgements in books to see how they should be written. Sometimes this section is placed at the end of the report.

Contents page
A contents page is essential for any report exceeding three pages. It should be on a separate sheet of paper and it should list the various sections of the report in the order in which they appear. The headings on the contents page must be identical to those used in the text, with the appropriate page (and/or paragraph) number alongside them. If you have used more than just one or two illustrations then provide a separate list of these below the section headings.

Your page numbering and paragraph numbering systems should be
simple and consistent (see Chapter 5).

Summary or Abstract or Synopsis
This component is particularly useful when you have a diverse
readership. It has two functions:

— To provide a précis of what the recipient is about to read or has
   just read.
— To provide an outline of the report if the recipient is not going
   to read the entire report.

An average manager's reading speed is between 200 and 250 words
per minute, and he or she comprehends only 75 percent of this. It
is therefore extremely important to highlight the **salient facts** and
the **main conclusions and recommendations**, if any. Obviously it
cannot be written until *after* the other components of the report.
Keep it concise; it should never exceed one page. Do not introduce
any matter which is not covered within the text of the report.

A summary *could* contain just five paragraphs:

- Intention (your purpose and scope)

- Outline (what was done and how it was done)

- Main findings

- Main conclusions

- Main recommendations (if necessary)

As a general rule, the more senior the reader, the less detail he or
she will require. For this reason a reader is sometimes sent a
summary *instead* of the entire report. When this is done the covering letter should offer a copy of the full report, if required.

Introduction
This section sets the scene. While the title page gives a broad
indication of the subject, the introduction tells the reader what it is
all about. A good introduction will engage the readers' interest and

will include everything that they will need to know before moving on to the main body of the report. It will contain certain essential preliminaries which would not be weighty enough individually to justify headings of their own. These might include:

- Why was the report written? Who requested it, and when?

- What were your terms of reference? *Always* refer to these in the introduction.

- What resources were available to you? (For example, staff, time and equipment.)

- What limitations, if any, did you work under? What were the reasons for this? (For example, 'The report does not analyse departmental expenditure in June because the figures were not available'.)

- What sources of information did you use? How did you obtain this information? (See Chapter 2.)

- What were your methods of working? A technical report will require a technical explanation of methods used. (Some writers prefer to provide this information in an appendix).

- How is the report structured? Why did you choose this method of presentation? This explanation helps your readers find their way around the report and shows the logic of the layout.

In some reports the first two of these preliminaries are called **aims** and the others are known collectively as **scope**.

Reports should not be anonymous documents, so it is usual for the name and signature of the author to appear immediately below the introduction. Some organisations prefer the signature to appear under the writer's name on the title page. Either way, it is best to sign every copy rather than simply sign and photocopy the master copy. In the case of professional firms preparing reports for clients, it is customary for only the name of the practice to be given. This indicates the joint responsibility of the partnership. The identity of the author is denoted by the reference.

Main body

As the name suggests, this section contains the main discussion of your subject-matter. It is very important to plan a sensible substructure for this section bearing in mind, once again:

- The requirements of the person who commissioned the report

- House-style

- Custom and convention

- Your objective(s)

- Your readership

- Common sense

There are three basic substructures to consider:

- the logical substructure,

- the sectional substructure, or

- the creative substructure.

The logical substructure

Here, procedures or events are discussed in the sequence in which they occur or occurred. Such a substructure would be suitable for a report which **instructs** (perhaps duty notes), or for a factual report which **explains** (perhaps how some event occurred). It is a very simple format but it can become boring, especially in lengthy reports or in reports requiring a large number of cross-references.

The sectional substructure

With this format the information is presented in meaningful sections. For example, an internal audit report could discuss the work of each department in turn, or it could perhaps deal with each engineering or clerical function in turn. This structure is useful when a report **describes** (perhaps how a system works); **informs** (perhaps how the various components of an overall project are progressing); **evaluates** (perhaps the performance of various projects, possibly leading to a recommendation as to which of them the company should purchase); or **provokes debate** (perhaps providing a series of discussion points on various topics to be debated at a future meeting). This format is particularly useful when readers are not likely to be interested in all your findings. Each of them can select one or more sections and read them in isolation. However, it is still important to provide links between these sections for the benefit of any reader who may decide to read the entire report.

The creative substructure
Information is presented in an *apparently* haphazard way. In a sense it is a hybrid of the other substructures and it is most commonly used in reports written to **persuade** (perhaps to convince people to buy your product). If such a report is written well it can be very effective. However, you should not attempt to use this imprecise substructure until you feel very confident about your report writing skills. Both good and bad writers sometimes break the rules, but only the good writers know the rules they are breaking and so are far more likely to get away with it.

Conclusions
Your conclusions should link your terms of reference (what you were trying to do, as stated in your introduction) with your findings (what you found out, as presented in your main body). They should flow naturally from your evidence and arguments; there must no surprises. Conclusions should always be:

- Clearly and simply stated

- Objective and not exaggerated

- Written with the likely impact on the reader clearly in mind

Recommendations
Do not make any recommendations unless your terms of reference empower you to do so. While conclusions refer to the *past* and/or the *present*, recommendations look to the *future*. Any comment not concerned with the future has no place as a recommendation. Your recommendations should follow logically from your conclusions. Therefore, once again, there should be no surprises.

Effective recommendations are brief and to the point. They are also specific. For example, management may need to know what should be done by whom to overcome a specific problem; it will not want to be told that some undefined action should be taken by some unidentified individual for no apparent reason. Your recommendations must also be realistic. Perhaps the security at a warehouse should be improved. If so, do not risk the rejection of a sensible recommendation, and the general undermining of the credibility of your report, by asking for too much. It is not really reasonable or feasible to expect it to be protected as thoroughly as Fort Knox. So think carefully about the implications of all your recommendations; talk to the people involved and, where necessary, try to come to sensible compromises. Jaw is better than war.

A good way to check whether your recommendations are well-written is to extract them from the rest of the report and then read them in isolation. Do they still make sense? If not, re-draft them until they do.

Appendixes
The purpose of an appendix is to supplement the information contained in the main body of the report. It is a way of providing adequate detail for readers who require it without breaking the thread of the main body. But how do you know what information to put in appendixes, what to include in the main body and what to exclude from the report altogether? Figure 1 is an example of an algorithm that will help you decide the answer.

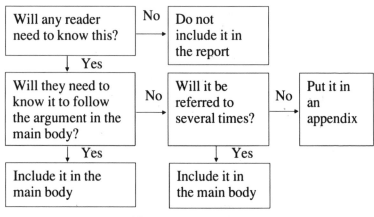

Figure 1. An algorithm

Appendixes are useful as a way of:

- Meeting the needs of a diverse readership – some people will want/need to refer to them while others will not;

- Substantiating and/or amplifying findings in the main body;

- Presenting documentary evidence to support arguments in the main body (for example, copies of memos, reports, correspondence, instructions, forms, standard letters, questionnaires, maps, charts and so on);

- Providing detailed results of experiments or investigations;

- Presenting summaries of results obtained elsewhere;

- Presenting statistical or comparative information;

- Illustrating relationships or relative proportions by means of charts and diagrams (see Chapter 8), and

- Explaining systems or procedures by flow charts and/or words (see Chapter 8).

An appendix is useless, however, unless it is clearly referred to in the main body of the report and in the contents list. *Tell* the readers why they may wish to refer to it.

References
This section provides full details of the books or journals which have been specifically mentioned in the text, or from which extracts have been quoted. They should be listed in the same order as referred to in the report. Details of books should follow this style:

Audrey Segal *Careers Encyclopaedia*,
13th ed, Cassell (1992)
or, *Careers Encyclopaedia*, Audrey Segal (Cassell, 13th edition, 1992)

Journals should be recorded in this way:

J.F.C. KINGMAN 'On The Algebra of Queues', *Methuen's Review Series in Applied Probability*, Vol 6, pp1-44 (1966)

Some report writers prefer to use footnotes rather than a reference section. They list each reference at the foot of the relevant page, the end of the relevant section or at the end of the report. This last method is very similar to providing a reference section.

Bibliography
A bibliography also gives full details of every publication referred to in the text. However, unlike a reference section, it may also include books and journals *not* referred to. A bibliography is useful when you have a diverse readership since you can provide separate lists for **Background reading, Further reading** and **Recommended reading**. Details of publications are given in the same format as are references, but it is customary to list them alphabetically by the surname of the author or by the title of the book.

Glossary
A glossary is necessary when you have used a good deal of specialised or technical vocabulary. It is another useful device to help meet the needs of a diverse readership, some of whom will be familiar with the terminology and some of whom will not be. Make sure your definitions are authoritative, precise and up-to-date (words come and go and some change their meaning over time). For this reason it is important that your dictionary or reference book is a current edition.

List the words alphabetically and place the section towards the end of the report. However, if a large number of readers will need to familiarise themselves with the vocabulary before reading the report, it is better to place the glossary at the beginning.

Index
An index is necessary only for a large report. It should contain more entries than a contents page and it is perfectly acceptable for it to be presented in two or three columns. List items alphabetically and place the index at the end of the report.

You've now seen that there are many factors to consider when selecting a suitable skeletal format. If you have not been given any guidance, and if your report is not one of the more common types discussed in Chapter 10, consider this simple format:

- Title page
- Contents page

- Summary
- Introduction
- Main body
- Conclusions
- Recommendations (if required)
- Appendixes

Put yourself in your reader's shoes; how would *they* like the report to be structured? Then critically examine your answer. Take each component in turn and ask yourself whether it is really necessary. For example: Is the title page necessary? The answer must be 'Yes' because it identifies the report to the reader. Or: Is the glossary necessary? If all your readers know (or at least are likely to know) the meaning of all the technical words you have used, the answer will be 'No'. In that case remove the glossary from the skeletal framework since it would serve no useful purpose.

A well-planned skeletal framework really is the key to effective report writing. It is of even greater value if a report is to be written by a number of people, because it:

- Enables each person to see the relationship between his or her contribution and the rest of the report;
- Provides detailed guidelines, thereby minimising the risk of omission or duplication; and
- Makes it easier to maintain a consistent approach.

In such cases, however, every contributor should be involved in preparing and finalising the skeletal framework to ensure that:

- Every necessary point will be covered;
- Each of these points is clearly understood; and
- Team spirit is fostered and maintained.

SUMMARY

It is essential to **prepare and plan** your report very carefully. As with most tasks, the amount of time and thought spent on these activities at this stage will make a vast difference to the effectiveness of all the work that will follow. It will also greatly enhance the appearance and professionalism of the report.

The key to good report writing is the preparation of a well-structured and appropriate **skeletal framework**. However, before you can construct such a framework you must be absolutely clear about:

- The precise purpose of the report

- Your overall objective(s)

- The nature of your readership

- The resources at your disposal

- The information you will need to gather

Only then can you begin to consider what combination of report **component parts** will be the most suitable to get your message across in the way you want.

This process of preparation and planning will greatly reduce the time and effort spent subsequently on writing and re-writing the report by:

- Reminding you of the message you will need to convey in order to get the results you want;

- Providing you with a logical and considered structure which will help you identify any gaps or illogicalities;

- Enabling you to obtain an overview of the entire report, thereby helping you maintain a sense of perspective; and

- Providing you with clear guidelines as you collect and handle the information, and then write the report.

2
Collecting and Handling Information

Once you have prepared and planned your report, it is time to carry out all the work that will be necessary before you can actually write it. In other words you are now undertaking your project or investigation. Your task is to collect and handle enough relevant information to be able to put flesh on the bones of your skeletal framework.

The following key questions now need to be addressed:

1. Where will I find the information I need?
2. How can I obtain information from these sources?
3. How should I record my findings?
4. How can I be sure the information is accurate and reliable?
5. How should I sort and group the information?

It is quite possible to write a bad report after doing good research, but it is impossible to write a good report after doing poor research. The moral is clear: good research is essential. Considering the questions above is a good starting-point for your research.

WHERE WILL I FIND THE INFORMATION I NEED?

By now you will have identified the information you will need, bearing in mind: the purpose of the report; your objective(s); the needs of your readers; your resources; your skeletal framework. Where, though, will you find this information?

There are four sources of information available to you:

- People
- Books and other publications
- Information technology and the media
- Events and places

The information you will need may be found under any or all these categories, so you might consider each in turn.

People
You may be able to obtain the information you require from the local, national, or even the international community. Here are some possibilities:

- Your colleagues
- Members of the public
- Politicians
- Producers
- Manufacturers
- Retailers
- Federations
- Unions
- Pressure groups
- International organisations

Books and other publications
Perhaps the information can be extracted from a printed source, such as:

- Encyclopaedias
- Reference books
- Text books
- Guides
- Handbooks
- Journals and magazines
- Newspapers
- Maps and charts
- Previous reports
- Correspondence
- Minutes

Information technology and the media
While it would be foolhardy to ignore the traditional sources of information listed above, it would be equally short-sighted not to take advantage of other relevant sources of information made possible by technological advances.

Videotex is the collective name for **teletext** and **viewdata**.

Teletext is broadcast information (Ceefax and Teletext 3 and Teletext 4). Viewdata is information transmitted along telephone lines (Prestel and Telecom Gold). Most of this kind of information is, by its very nature, subject to continual revision.

It is also possible to access the databases of other computers – even ones outside the UK. If you feel such information would be valuable, refer to the current edition of *How to Find Out Printed and On-Line Sources*, by George Chandler (Pergamon Press).

You can also make use of television, radio, video and pre-recorded audio material. All of these can provide information on a wide range of subjects.

Events and places

Depending on the purpose of your report, the information you require could be available at one or more events or places. Here is a small sample of local, national or international possibilities:

- Laboratories
- Libraries
- Research institutions
- Exhibitions
- Museums
- Galleries
- Cinemas
- Theatres
- Concerts
- Talks

HOW CAN I OBTAIN INFORMATION FROM THESE SOURCES?

Information can be gathered by one or more of these methods:

- Experimentation
- Reading
- Listening
- Observation
- Interview
- Letter
- Telephone call
- Questionnaire

Experimentation

An experiment should be carried out by a trained scientist who will design and perform it in an acceptable way. The experiment should be written up as follows:

- Begin with a dated heading stating clearly the **objective of the experiment**: 'To study . . .', 'To find . . .'.

- Give a brief account of the **theory** underlying the experiment.

- Provide a **hypothesis** (suggested answer), if you have one.

- Give a clear and full account of **how the experiment was carried out**. It is usually necessary to provide a **diagram** of the apparatus used.

- Provide a complete list of the **readings** you obtained.

- Provide a full **statement of the final result**, showing the estimated limits of error.

- **Conclude** with a clear and concise statement of what your results lead you to infer or deduce about the problem posed. If you have a hypothesis, refer to it here. If you have any relevant views on the experiment or the result obtained, include these. Also, if you believe that the experiment could have been improved in some way, explain why and how.

Reading

The way you read should vary according to the **complexity** of the material and the **reasons** for reading it. If you are reading to understand, absorb or master a topic you must read it slowly. If you are reading a novel for entertainment you can read it quickly.

Try the SQ3R method of reading:

S   Survey
Q   Question
R   Read
R   Recall
R   Review

Survey

This is the preliminary review of the book or article. It involves skimming (glancing over the material and getting the feel of it) and scanning (looking at specific aspects of the publication – the title, the author, the date, the preface, the introduction, the contents, any chapter summaries and the index). In the case of a book, it is also a good idea to read the first and last paragraphs of potentially relevant chapters and the first and last sentences of a sample of paragraphs within these chapters. This scanning should give you an overall impression of the publication, such as:

● Is it pitched at the right level?

● Is it up to date?

● Is the author a recognised authority in the field?

● Is the book factual or based on opinion?

Question

Then ask yourself these questions:

● What would I expect to gain if I read some or all of this material?

● Is some or all of the material directly relevant to my report?

● Does some or all of it provide a useful background to my report?

Read

Once you have decided to read some or all of a publication, divide your reading into manageable segments, probably chapters or sections. Read any summaries or conclusions *first*. Next read the chapter or section quickly to get a grasp of the material. Finally, read it again, more slowly, and ensure you understand it.

Recall

Think about the main ideas and facts you have been reading about and make notes of them (see How should I record my findings? p 44).

Review
Are you satisfied that you have gained what you expected through your reading? Have you gathered the information you will need to help put the flesh on your skeletal framework?

Listening

Some researchers suggest that we function at only 25 percent efficiency and rarely remember what we have heard. In one investigation the proportion of information which was correctly transmitted from a senior director through middle and line management to operative staff was as low as 20 percent. Such ineffective listening can be responsible for the following:

- Accidents at work

- Production breakdowns

- Lost sales and customers

- Poor morale

- Personality clashes

- Inaccurate communication

So how can you improve your listening skills?

Do not:

- assume that the topic is boring or irrelevant. A good listener sifts, screens and hunts for relevant information.

- criticise delivery or presentation; concentrate on the content.

- submit to emotional phrases. Do not allow the use of phrases which you loathe reduce your listening capacity.

- become overstimulated. Do not try to think of 'clever' or embarrassing questions. Use your time positively, listening and structuring your thoughts.

- listen only to facts. Think also of the main ideas, concepts, structure and how the values, attitudes and prejudices of the speaker affect the presentation.

- expect the speaker to structure the talk to suit your needs. As you take notes, follow the speaker's approach, otherwise your structure will not fit in with the concepts and ideas presented. You can rearrange your notes later.

- remain passive. Listening is an active process, so stay alert.

- tolerate distractions. If you cannot hear the speaker, or if you are too hot or too cold, then say so.

- listen to only what you want to hear. Be willing to consider arguments and evidence which oppose your views. Be aware of your prejudices.

- evade difficult subjects. Face problems head on.

- waste your thinking potential. People normally **talk** at about 125 words per minute, but they **listen** and can **think** at about 400 words per minute. The differential of 275 words per minute is a breeding ground for day dreaming.

Do:

- run ahead of the speaker. What has been said? What might be said? What is this all leading to? What are the implications of this message? By asking yourself these questions you will improve your concentration.

- examine the evidence presented. Is it accurate, objective and complete? Is it strong or weak? (see How can I be sure the information is accurate and reliable? page 47).

- recap every few minutes in order to avoid day dreaming.

- remember that listening is an active process and is therefore very hard work.

```
Traffic Passing Anytown Primary School (west – east)

Tally sheet no.:
Date:
Time:
Name of observer:

                                        | No. | % |
Cars                                    |     |   |
Buses                                   |     |   |
Lorries                                 |     |   |
Vans                                    |     |   |
Motor Bikes                             |     |   |
Push Bikes                              |     |   |
Other (specify)                         |     |   |
Total                                   |     |   |
```

Figure 2. A tally sheet

You have two ears and one mouth. Try to use them in roughly that proportion.

Observation

Sometimes the best way to find out is simply to observe. For example, you may be trying to find out how much traffic passes Anytown Primary School. According to your purpose you might need to break this figure down to the types of vehicle, specific days, and possibly to different times of year. The simplest way of recording your results is to use a series of tally sheets like the one illustrated in Figure 2.

Interview

Interviewing is a skilled technique and few people do it well. While the interview should appear to be reasonably casual, it must be planned and structured. Follow these key steps:

Step 1   Greet the interviewee in a friendly manner. Avoid too much small talk and maintain a professional image.

Step 2   Explain the precise purpose of the interview. What do you want to find out? Let the interviewee know that his or her input will be valued.

Step 3   Ask your questions. Use open questions (who, what, when, why, where, how), and try to avoid yes/no answers. Listen and show you understand. Then follow up with secondary questions. Give the interviewee time to answer. Cover one topic at a time; try not to 'hop about'. Empathise – do not judge or be seen to take sides.

Step 4   Sum up the interview to check your understanding of facts, opinions and circumstances.

Step 5   Thank the interviewee for his or her cooperation.

Letter

If you decide to ask for information by letter, remember to:

- Name the person you are writing to and give his or her designation and organisation (for example, Miss V. Rich, Chief Finance Officer, Midshire County Council).

- Give the letter a heading.

- Explain the purpose of your report in the first paragraph.

- Courteously ask for the information you require. Keep it concise but comprehensive.

- If possible, draw a table where this information can be inserted.

- Send the letter as early as possible and tactfully request a reply within two or three weeks.

- Enclose a stamped addressed envelope.

- Conclude the letter by thanking the person in anticipation.

Telephone call

Sometimes you can obtain the information you need by making one or more telephone calls. However this method is not recommended when the information is likely to be fairly complex and/or there are figures involved (for example, 'Did she say £4, £14, or £40?').

Telephone calls are most appropriate when you know the person and when your questions are straightforward (often requiring no more than yes/no answers).

If you do decide to telephone, write down the questions you want to ask and have a pen and a few sheets of paper handy. If you are using a public call box, make sure you have plenty of change with you. Then follow these key steps:

Step 1   Give your name ('Good morning, I'm . . .').

Step 2   Ask for the right person ('May I speak to . . .').

Step 3   Explain why you are telephoning. Emphasise that you are not selling anything! ('I'm phoning about a report I am preparing on . . .').

Step 4   Politely ask for the information you require. Let them know that their input will be appreciated ('I would be extremely grateful if you could help me on one or two points . . .').

Step 5   Thank the person by name.

Speak distinctly, deliberately and a little more slowly than you normally do. Make your voice pleasant, cheerful and positive. Keep the conversation as brief as possible without ever being abrupt.

Questionnaire

This method of information gathering involves questioning a sample of people (respondents). Questionnaires seek two kinds of information:

- **Factual.** For example, 'How often do you *buy* Product A?'

- **Opinion.** For example, 'What do you *think* of Product A?'

Such a survey is necessary only if the information sought is not already available, or if the information is out of date. There are two important points to bear in mind when producing a questionnaire. First, you will need to approach members of the public and they have no obligation to assist you, so check that your questions (and your general approach) are courteous. Second, make sure that your questions are relevant to the subject of your report.

Figure 3 is an example of a simple questionnaire about school meals (adapted from a questionnaire in *How to Succeed at GCSE*, John Bowden, Cassell 1989).

Here is a checklist for a good questionnaire:

- Does it have a title?
- Does it have a reference or questionnaire number?
- Does it record the name of the interviewer?
- Is it well spaced?
- Does it explain the purpose of the questionnaire?
- Where appropriate, does it emphasise that all replies will be treated confidentially?
- Is it clear and unambiguous?
- Is it simple?
- Is it logically developed?
- Does it ask one question at a time (not two or more questions at the same time)?
- Does it require definite answers?
- Does it avoid leading questions? (Ask: 'What do you think of product A?' not: 'Product A is fantastic. Do you agree?'.)
- Does it avoid an appeal to vanity? (Ask: 'Do you take regular exercise?', not: 'Most fit people exercise regularly. Do you?'.)
- Does it avoid an appeal to sympathy? (Ask: 'Should the Health Service be better funded?', not: 'People are dying needlessly. Should the National Health Service be better funded?').
- Where appropriate, does it leave sensitive areas until last (for example, the age of middle-aged or elderly respondents)?
- Is the questionnaire written in such a way that will make it straightforward to record and analyse your overall results?
- Has the questionnaire been 'pilot tested' among a small number of respondents to highlight any obvious errors, omissions, ambiguities and other shortcomings before the survey goes live?

School Meals Questionnaire

Questionnaire No.   Interviewer:
                                           Date:

'I am carrying out a survey on school meals on behalf of Midshire County Council. I wonder whether you would be willing to answer a few questions?'

Ask the respondent

Q 1   Which class are you in?   First year   ☐
                                          Second year   ☐
                                          Third year   ☐
                                          Fourth year   ☐
                                          Fifth year   ☐
                                          Sixth year   ☐

Q 2   Enter the sex of the respondent   Male   ☐
                                          Female   ☐

Q 3   How often do you have school meals? Every day   ☐
                                          Most days   ☐
                                          2 or 3 days per week ☐
                                          Not often   ☐
                                          Never   ☐

If the answer is 'Every day', go staight to Q 5

Q 4   When you don't have a school dinner,
      what do you do instead?   Go home to dinner   ☐
                                          Buy dinner elsewhere ☐
                                          Bring own food   ☐
                                          Have no dinner   ☐
                                          Other (specify)   ☐

Q 5   Do you think that school meals are: Very good?   ☐
                                          Quite good?   ☐
                                          Average?   ☐
                                          Bad?   ☐
                                          Awful?   ☐

Thank respondent for helping

Figure 3. A questionnaire

Once you have designed your questionnaire and amended it as necessary, you must decide on sampling methods. No strict rules can be laid down for sampling. The methods used will depend on the circumstances of the case, but unless the methods are **random** the reliability of the results is no more than a matter of opinion.

The following are three common sampling techniques:

Simple random sampling
This is a quick and simple method, by which every person or item has an equal chance of being selected. If you want to select 10 per cent of a population of 100, simply take ten names out of a hat containing the 100 names.

Systematic random sampling
Again, every person or item has an equal chance of being selected, but the choice is made to a prearranged plan (though it is still random). For example, select every 100th name on the electoral register.

Quota sampling
This is used to get a balanced view from people in the street based on age, sex and possibly social class. For example, select twenty males, aged 16-20; twenty males, 21-25; twenty males, 26-30; twenty females, 16-20; twenty females, 21-25; twenty females, 26-30.

Finally you should be aware of **errors that can occur** owing to **bias** in sampling or questioning. Here are some ways of avoiding bias:

In sampling:

• Do not **deliberately** select people or items. All selections must be **random**.

• Do not substitute or replace items selected randomly. For example, if you decide to question somebody from every twentieth house, do not change to the twenty-first if you do not receive a reply at the twentieth. The house-holders may be at work and should not be excluded for this reason. Call at a different time or on a different day.

- Do not deliberately omit items that should be selected randomly. If you need to select ten males, aged 16-20, approach a random selection – not, for instance, just young professionals.

In questioning:

- Do not vary the wording of your questions.

- Do not ask leading questions.

- Do not ask questions which appeal to vanity.

- Do not ask questions which appeal to sympathy.

HOW SHOULD I RECORD MY FINDINGS?

Many organisations have their own formal systems for recording information. For example, report writers may be expected to produce working papers which may be reviewed before, during or after the production of a report. These papers may also need to be consulted if any statement in that report is challenged, or if some clarification is required. Some organisations will require files of background information, or planning information, or progress reports, or staff and other resource usage and costs, or documents required to generate data. So **ultimately** you must record your findings in the way your organisation prescribes.

However, you may have more freedom to choose the methods by which you record your findings **during** the investigation or project. There are many ways of doing this, and each person will prefer a particular method. Here we shall briefly examine two methods of note-taking:

- Traditional notes and

- Patterned notes

Traditional notes
In this method of note-taking, material is condensed using headings and subheadings, and then emphasising the most important points or arguments. This method is also the basis of report writing.

When you make traditional notes, use loose-leaf paper, double spacing, write on one side of the paper only and leave generous margins. This will allow notes to be rearranged and added to when required. You must also decide the layout which suits you best, but remember that it must be as clear and comprehensive as possible. Here are a few suggestions:

- Once you have chosen a layout, stick to it.

- Use a consistent numbering system (see Chapter 5).

- Use diagrams and illustrations as well as writing (see Chapter 8).

- Use abbreviations, but be clear, simple and consistent. For example:

Omit syllables	–	Expt (Experiment)
Abbreviate endings	–	Exptg (Experimenting)
Omit unnecessary words	–	the, a, an
Use initials	–	Pres. (President)

- Also use recognised abbreviations like these:

e.g.	for example
cf.	compare
∴	therefore
bc	because
→	it follows
viz.	namely
i.e.	that is
no.	number
=	equals
w/	with
w/o	without
q.v.	see
p.	page
b/4	before
ref.	reference
etc.	etcetera

Patterned notes

In his book *Use Your Head,* Tony Buzan describes an alternative type of note-taking which allows you to summarise your understanding and helps you find links between information and ideas. You start your patterned notes in the centre of a page and your ideas spray out from it. The best way to illustrate this is to give an example. Suppose you were asked to produce a report on the sources of information available to the report writer (see page 31: **Where will I find the information I need?).** You might plan the report by using patterned notes to help you identify the relevant ideas, concepts and facts which you already know, and those you will need to find out. Your patterned notes could be built up until they look something like Figure 4.

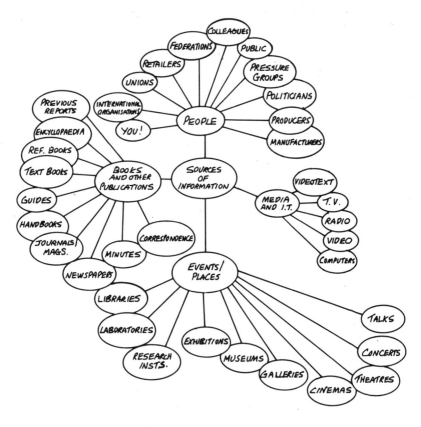

Figure 4. Patterned notes

There are some clear advantages in using patterned notes:

- They let you see the whole picture.

- They are very flexible (you can add to them).

- They highlight links.

- They remind you what you already know and what you will need to find out.

- They are quicker to write.

- They are quicker to read.

- They help you plan your report.

However, they can become over elaborate and confusing. Also, they are not very suitable for displaying just facts rather than ideas, concepts and facts. So do not neglect traditional notes, but seriously consider using patterned notes as well.

Whichever method of note-taking you use, remember that good notes will always follow the '5C' rule – they will be:

- Clear

- Concise

- Comprehensive

- Complete and

- Correct.

HOW CAN I BE SURE THE INFORMATION IS ACCURATE AND RELIABLE?

Obviously this will depend on the type of information you have collected. However, regardless of the source of information, there is always the possibility of some kind of biased representation.

Chapter 4 examines some aspects of thinking; this will not only help you avoid some of the more common faults in thinking, it will also help you detect faults in other people's thinking. However, at this stage, you should be aware of the four factors by which information should be judged, namely its:

- Accuracy
- Objectivity
- Completeness and
- Strength.

Accuracy

Sometimes you can check the data supplied. For example, are the **mathematical calculations** accurate? If there are too many to check, remember Pareto's principle which states that 80 percent of what is important is represented by 20 percent of what exists. Concentrate on this 20 percent. **Information** may also be inaccurate if it is out of date. In **experimental work**, was current equipment used? In **legal matters**, has account been taken of any recent and relevant legislation or case law? When **text books** have been consulted, were they the most recent editions?

Objectivity

When people have strongly held beliefs they will often see or hear things which support these beliefs, but they will not see or hear things which oppose them. For example, self-deception may cause results to be interpreted incorrectly. Going further, it is not unknown for people to perpetrate fraud, either to hoax or to provide 'evidence' to support pre-conceived ideas.

So ask yourself whether all the **major or relevant points of view** have been fairly represented. If the subject is controversial, the arguments for both (or all) cases should have been presented. At the very least, the person who provided the information should have made it clear that the views expressed are his or her own, and should then provide references to opposing viewpoints.

Finally, be very wary of statements without supporting evidence.

Completeness

In computer science a 'hash total' is used to ensure the completeness of a batch of records. However, it is often extremely difficult to prove that information is complete or, more accurately, that it is not incomplete. For example, we know of many animals that once inhabited the world. But how can we prove that they were the only ones? How can we prove that unicorns never existed? What you must ask yourself, therefore, is whether **all relevant information** has been provided and whether any attempt has been made to deceive or mislead by omission. Then look at it from the other side: is all the information provided relevant or is someone trying to 'blind you with science'?

Strength

Evidence is strong when:

- It can be verified or re-performed (for example, a scientific experiment),
- Independent observers have all come to the same conclusion,
- There have been a large number of consistent observations, and
- It is in agreement with the general body of knowledge.

Conversely, evidence is weak when some or all of these conditions cannot be satisfied. Always differentiate between fact and opinion, and remember that the former provides the stronger evidence.

HOW SHOULD I SORT AND GROUP THE INFORMATION?

It is important to sort and group your findings sensibly so that your notes remain manageable. If the report has been well-planned, this process will be quite straightforward. Use the **headings** and **sub-headings** of your **skeletal framework** (see Chapter 1), and make sure that you have gathered enough relevant information to complete *each* section and sub-section of this structure.

If you need more information, gather it now – not once you have started to draft your report. However, remember that your framework is a means to an end – to help you get your message across, and in the way you need to get it across – it is not an end in itself. Perhaps some particularly important findings will need to be highlighted. If so do not be afraid to amend your framework. You will not have wasted your time, because your original skeletal framework will have provided an essential overall structure for your investigation or project. Not only that, it is far easier to amend a framework at this stage than to attempt to create one for the first time.

SUMMARY

While it is quite possible to write a bad report after completing a good investigation or project, it is *impossible* to write a good report until you have successfully **identified, collected, recorded, evaluated,** and **sorted and grouped** the right amount of relevant information.

There are four sources of information available to you:

- People

- Books and other publications

- Information technology and the media

- Events and places

Information can be gathered from these sources by one or more of the following methods:

- Experimentation

- Reading

- Listening

- Observation

- Interview

- Letter

- Telephone call

- Questionnaire

As you collect your information you should record it in traditional note form and/or in patterned notes. Whichever method(s) you use, your notes should follow the '5C' rule: they should be:

- Clear

- Concise

- Comprehensive

- Complete and

- Correct

Then critically evaluate the evidence and arguments. Are they:

- Accurate?

- Objective?

- Complete? and

- Strong?

Once you are satisfied about the accuracy and reliability of the information, ask yourself whether your skeletal framework remains the best structure to get your **desired message** across as you need to. If necessary amend it until it is. Then make sure you have gathered enough relevant information to complete each section and subsection of your (revised) framework. Finally, sort and group your information to match this final framework.

This process of collecting and handling information will greatly reduce the time spent subsequently on writing and re-writing the report, since you will need only to 'put flesh on the bones'. You can therefore now concentrate on the writing itself.

3
Writing the Report

Paradoxically, for a book about producing a report, this chapter is one of the shortest. The reason for this is simple. If sufficient thought has been devoted to preparing and planning (and possibly revising) the skeletal framework (Chapter 1), and to collecting and handling the information (Chapter 2), you will now have a practical blueprint for the entire report. Writing will entail amplifying the points in each section and 'putting flesh on the bones'.

The highly subjective and mentally demanding process of written communication is the subject of Chapter 6. This chapter considers the *clinical* process of writing (the order and the stages of writing) by answering these questions:

1. In what order should I write the first draft?

2. How should I write and review the main body and appendixes?

3. How should I write and review the Conclusions, Recommendations, Introduction and Summary?

4. Who should check and amend the first draft?

5. What final checks should I make before the report is issued?

Try answering each of these in turn. . .

IN WHAT ORDER SHOULD I WRITE THE FIRST DRAFT?

The order of writing is important. The **main body** and any **appendixes** should be written first. The other sections of the report should not be drafted until these have been completed, reviewed and, where necessary, re-drafted.

HOW SHOULD I WRITE AND REVIEW THE MAIN BODY AND APPENDIXES?

You will be aware in the back of your mind that this draft is likely to be amended. This is not a reason to treat it lightly. The better your first draft, the better will be your final draft. So write as if *this* is your final draft.

Starting to write

The important thing now is to start writing. For any writer there is little worse than the horror of facing that blank page. So begin with any section or subsection of the main body, or with any appendix. Choose one which you feel particularly confident about. It doesn't matter which you choose – just start writing!

However, don't try to write too much, too quickly. Most people work best in bursts of twenty to forty minutes. After that their concentration wavers and the quality of their writing suffers. So write a section, subsection or appendix and then take a short break. If this is not possible (unfortunately some employers are more concerned with the number of hours you put in rather than with what you put into the hours), do some work unconnected with the report. Then return to your writing and draft another section, subsection or appendix.

Once you have completed the main body and the appendixes, try to forget about them for a while. Distance yourself from them. If this is impracticable, at least leave it until after lunch or your tea break. Then come back with a fresh mind. Assess what you have *actually written* and how it *comes across*, rather than still thinking about what you had intended to write and get across.

Criticise Yourself

Put yourself in your readers' shoes and be highly self-critical. As you re-read your work you should:

- assess whether the substructure of the main body (logical, sectional or creative – see Chapter 1) is really the most suitable one to present your facts and arguments;
- examine the layout and general appearance;
- determine whether the tone and balance are correct;
- review the use and format of tabulations and appendixes;
- check the accuracy of figures and calculations; and
- check the use of English, punctuation and spelling.

This self-assessment should give you an idea of whether it's necessary to re-structure your framework and/or re-write any of the main body or appendixes, in order to get your message across as you had intended. If it is, do so.

HOW SHOULD I WRITE AND REVIEW THE CONCLUSIONS, RECOMMENDATIONS, INTRODUCTION AND SUMMARY?

Once any necessary amendments have been made to the main body and appendixes, the other sections of the report can be written. Each of these can now be directly related to what has *actually* been written in the main body and appendixes. Most writers draft them in the same order as they appear in the question above. If you wish to be reminded about the information required in each section or component (and also in other less common components), refer to Chapter 1. Remember that your **conclusions** must follow logically from your **findings**, and your **recommendations** must follow logically from your conclusions. Your introduction should include everything that your readers will need to know before they read the rest of the report.

While these sections are all important, you must pay particular attention to your **summary**. Make sure that the overall opinion, expressed accurately, reflects the findings and comments given in the main body and appendixes. It must be a true summary of the report and it should highlight any areas requiring a particular emphasis. As already stated, the summary should stimulate the readers' interests by outlining:

- The salient facts

- The main conclusions and recommendations

Remember that it must serve two overall functions:

- To provide a précis of what the recipient is going to read or has just read.

- To provide an outline of the report if the recipient is not going to read any more of the report.

If the reader finds the summary boring, the report will fail.

Once you have written the entire report, try to forget it for a few days – or at least for a few hours. Then re-read it. Does it flow? Are there adequate links and signposts for the reader? Would *you* be convinced by the arguments? Could you justify everything that you have written, if necessary? Finally, ask yourself whether you would be willing to *say* what you have *written* to the recipients, face to face. If you would not be willing to say it, do not write it either.

Now send the draft to the typist or printer.

WHO SHOULD CHECK AND AMEND THE FIRST DRAFT?

It is usual for three people to be involved in checking and amending a first draft:

- Yourself

- A colleague

- Your line manager

When the draft is returned, re-read it very carefully. Make a note of the following:

- Errors made by the typist or printer.

- Errors made by you.

- Examples of poor presentation, including unrequired or inconsistent:

> variations in the size and style of lettering,
> headings and subheadings,
> numbering,
> highlighting techniques,
> margins and spacing.

You will find a list of standard proof correction marks in the current edition of the *Writers' and Artists' Yearbook.*

It is far easier to spot mistakes and other shortcomings on a typed document than on a manuscript, so ask yourself whether every

section, subsection, paragraph, sentence and word is really justified. Are they all necessary? Do they convey the meaning you
intended? Are they accurate? Amend the report as necessary.

However, by now you will have read and re-read the draft so
often that you may not be able to see the wood from the trees. So
ask a sympathetic and knowledgeable colleague to give his or her
candid comments on the report. It is far easier to detect flaws in
other people's writing than in your own. Are there any obvious
errors or **ambiguities**? What changes or improvements would they
suggest? What impact is it all likely to have on your readers? (You
have been too closely involved with the report to objectively judge
its impact.) Amend the report as necessary.

Now pass the report to your **line manager**. As well as asking the
same sorts of question about it as you and your colleague did, your
line manager will probably be considering wider aspects of the
report:

- its technical content,

- its overall relevance, and

- whether it is politically sensitive.

If the report was authorised by a senior officer, your line manager
will be particularly concerned that it does not discredit anyone
within his or her department.

It is likely that you will be asked questions about the report. You
should be told why any changes are made. Unfortunately, this does
not always happen. Try to find out. If your manager is too busy to
tell you now, ask if you may discuss it later. This is in both your
interests. You will learn some valuable lessons and your manager
should need to make fewer amendments to your next report.

The Final Draft

By now this draft will have so many comments and amendments
on it that it will almost certainly need to be re-typed. This is likely
to be the final draft. After three drafts it is probable that the report
will not get any better anyway. Re-writing to get it right is an
excellent practice; re-writing as a matter of course is a very bad and
wasteful practice.

In some organisations the final draft is circulated to key readers *before* the report is finalised. In this way the writer will get their initial reactions and may well decide to amend the draft to include some or all of their ideas. They will probably point out any obvious errors and they will be more likely to support the final version. If you do circulate a draft report, make sure it is clearly annotated 'Draft' on the cover and on every page. Give all comments due consideration, but do not amend the report simply because some of the recipients do not like your findings. Remain objective.

WHAT FINAL CHECKS SHOULD I MAKE BEFORE THE REPORT IS ISSUED?

Before you send your fair copy – or final (revised) copy – for typing, it is essential for the typist to know precisely what is required. For example, will he or she be expected to add the page numbers to the contents page or will that component be typed separately later? What style and size of lettering will be required? The importance of working closely with the typist is discussed in Chapter 5.

The importance of proofreading
When the typing is returned, it must be proof-checked in great detail. What does this say?

Paris
in the
the spring

If you were proofreading this chapter, you would be expected to have spotted the extra 'the'.

Regardless of the time and effort put into writing the report, the required result will not be achieved without sufficient care being devoted to this process of proofreading. A poorly typed report, full of errors and inconsistencies in layout, has a damaging effect regardless of the quality of the content. Typing mistakes, therefore, must be identified and corrected; there really is no excuse for failing to do this properly.

If the report has been typed on a **word processor**, layout is straightforward, but it is possible for it to be adversely affected by changes made to the draft report, which will have been **saved on disc**. For example, a heading could come at the foot of a page, or a table or paragraph could be split between two pages on the revised version because a line of text has been deleted from the first document, or because a block of text has been moved. This gives a bad impression and emphasises the importance of careful typing and proofreading before the report is issued.

Final touches

The responsibility for **final approval** of the report often rests with the writer's manager. Once this approval has been obtained, arrange for or make the correct number of bound copies, including at least one for file (see Chapter 9 for a discussion of covers and bindings). By publication day the names, addresses and designations of all the recipients should be known and checked. Envelopes, wrappers and labels should have been made up, covering letters or compliment slips prepared to explain why the report has been sent and to provide a contact point (probably you) if further enquiry or comment is desired. Any reply cards should have been typed.

Record full details of all issues in a register and make sure that every person receives his or her copy at the same time.

SUMMARY

If sufficient thought has been devoted to preparing and planning the skeletal framework, and to collecting and handling the information, writing the report will be reasonably straightforward. You will need to amplify the points in each section of the framework, and 'put flesh on the bones'.

The key stages of report writing are:

1. Drafting the main body and appendixes.

2. Reviewing and amending the main body and appendixes.

3. Drafting the Conclusions, Recommendations, Introduction, Summary, and any other report component used.

4. Reviewing and amending these components.

5. Getting the draft typed.

6. Checking and amending the draft.

7. Asking a colleague to comment on the draft and amending the draft if necessary.

8. Passing the draft to your line manager, to amend it or tell you how to amend it.

9. Re-writing the report, if necessary.

10. Explaining to the typist precisely what is required and having it typed.

11. Checking the typing, and having it corrected, if necessary.

12. Seeking approval to issue the report.

13. Arranging for or making the correct number of bound copies.

14. Issuing the report with compliment slips or covering letters, and recording full details of these issues in a register.

4
Improving Your Thinking

Thinking can be defined as the exercise of the mind in order to make a judgement or a decision.

This chapter considers two questions:

1. How can I make a reasoned judgement or decision?

2. What common faults in thinking should I avoid?

HOW CAN I MAKE A REASONED JUDGEMENT OR DECISION?

This demands clear and critical thinking.

Clear thinking
This is the ability to consider a matter objectively, ignoring everything except relevant information. In order to think clearly you must:

- Know precisely what you are trying to do and why you are trying to do it.

- Understand the evidence.

- Consider alternative relevant evidence.

- Consider the topic from all possible sides – is the evidence balanced?

- Look at the examples quoted – are they typical?

- Recognise that there will be a variety of interconnected

causes for, and consequences of, an event. These causes and consequences will not be of equal importance.

- Differentiate between facts and opinions.

- Appreciate motives – when and why was a source of information produced? – and realise that different people will have different views, which will be affected by their ideas, social and economic situation, religion, political beliefs, perceived interests, and so on.

- Be aware of the dangers of generalisations.

Critical thinking is the ability to come to a reasoned judgement on any matter. It can be considered as a seven-stage process:

1. Define the problem.
2. Formulate hypotheses and possible solutions.
3. Search for evidence and relevant facts.
4. Make inferences and draw logical conclusions from these facts.
5. Verify your conclusions.
6. Make logical recommendations from these conclusions.
7. Confirm the feasibility of these recommendations.

We have already discussed the first three stages in some detail. Your **problem** is defined by your terms of reference. Your **hypotheses and possible solutions** are formulated after due consideration of:

- your overall purpose;

- your objective(s);

- the nature of your readership;

- your limited resources.

What message will you need to convey; and how will you need to convey it (what is your skeletal framework)? Once you have formulated possible solutions you must identify and then collect enough **relevant information** to make your solutions possible.

Inference means going beyond a particular set of facts and concluding that they imply other facts. If you saw a man running along a pavement, you could not infer very much from that. However, if he is being pursued by a police officer who is blowing a whistle, you could reasonably infer that he is suspected of having committed some offence.

Your **conclusions** should follow the evidence presented in the main body of the report. There should be no surprises. Refer to your terms of reference (your problem) and then look for patterns and consistency in the evidence (or perhaps a lack of patterns and consistency) to arrive at your conclusions – your verdict.

Verification is the action or process of confirming or testing the truth or accuracy of a proposition. Be a devil's advocate. Are your conclusions reasonable, based on all the evidence available? Take arguments to extremes. This may disclose errors or generalisations. For example, recently I read this conclusion: 'Security at the factory is non-existent'. Non-existent? Surely not. Were there no locks, no fences, no security checks? The security may well have been very unsatisfactory, but it could not have been non-existent.

If you are required to make any **recommendations**, it is essential that they follow logically from your conclusions. Think carefully about them and then make them precise (*who* should do *what, when,* and *how*?). The question of *why* they should do it must be evident from the conclusions. As you formulate your recommendations think about what should happen in the future to alleviate any problems highlighted in your conclusions.

The final step is to **confirm that these recommendations are feasible**. In an ideal world there are probably many things that *should* happen in order to improve the situation – but in an ideal world the problems would not exist in the first place. In the real world resources are finite and therefore priorities must be set. So concentrate on significant issues. Put yourself in the shoes of the recipient. Are your recommendations feasible? Are they reasonable? Are they cost-effective? Are they practical? If they are not, do not make them.

WHAT COMMON FAULTS IN THINKING SHOULD I AVOID?

Here are some examples of common faults to be avoided. They

include a number of **fallacies**, which are arguments involving invalid forms of reasoning.

Selecting untypical examples
In 1991 the athlete Mike Powell jumped over 29 feet. This fact, however, does not give a great deal of support to an argument that we need never build a bridge unless a river is more than 29 feet wide.

Describing non-existent causal relationships
Since the early 1950s the yearly increase in juvenile crime has been almost identical to the increase in sales of ballpoint pens.

However, there is no reason to believe that the two trends are in any way connected.

Relying on experts
'Of course it's true, Professor Smith says so'.

The good professor may well be correct, but his or her arguments need to be tested just as rigorously as anyone else's before they are accepted. Also, as any Crown Court judge will testify, it is often possible to cite an equally eminent authority with an absolutely opposing view.

Exceeding the evidence
In 1989 the spacecraft Voyager II discovered two moons around Neptune. The following day a leading national newspaper wrote: '... this tells us other planets will have moons yet to be discovered'. Not necessarily.

Presenting tautological statements
Here the same thing is said twice whilst giving the appearance of an argument. For example, 'People with high IQs do well in tests set by MENSA'.

This is hardly surprising because MENSA tests are *designed* to reveal people with high IQs.

The fallacy of the undistributed middle
Here the conclusion is invalid because it cannot be deduced from the first two premises, even if both are correct. For example:

Communists claim to repudiate racial discrimination. Prince Charles claims to repudiate racial discrimination. Therefore Prince Charles is a Communist.

The fallacy of division

This is the error of arguing from the fact that something is true of a thing considered as a whole that the same is true of the parts of that whole. For example:

> All our workers could complete the order by next Tuesday (that is, collectively)

does *not* mean that every single worker, individually, could complete the order by next Tuesday.

The fallacy of composition

This is the opposite of the previous fallacy.

> In the chaos anyone could have escaped (that is, singularly),

does *not* mean that everyone could have escaped.

The fallacy of many questions

Here the mistake is putting or accepting a question that takes for granted a false answer to some prior question or questions. For example:

> When will it be convenient for me to visit you?

presupposes that you are *going* to visit.

The converse fallacy of accident

This is the error of arguing from a qualified principle or statement to an unqualified one. For example:

> You will be given the order if you can guarantee these delivery dates

does *not* mean:

> You will be given the order.

The gambler's fallacy

This is the mistaken belief that a run of bad luck will always be followed by a run of good luck (and vice versa). For example:

> There is no point in insuring the building this year; lightning never strikes twice.

The genetic fallacy

Here the error is in arguing that because something is now such-and-such, it must therefore have been such-and-such at any earlier date; or because it was such-and-such then, therefore it must be the same now. For example:

XYZ is a fine company. I remember the excellent last lot of work they did for us, in 1970.

The masked man fallacy

This is the mistake of arguing that because someone knows (or does not know) something under one description, they must therefore know it (or therefore cannot know it) as the same thing when it appears under another description. For example:

I know Fred, and I do not know who phoned me at 3 o'clock this morning,

does *not* mean that Fred did not phone me.

Affirming the consequent or denying the antecedent

If he got the job he'll be in the pub.

This does *not* mean:

- That if he is in the pub he necessarily got the job, or:

- That if he did not get the job that he will not be in the pub.

What it *does* mean is:

- That if he got the job he will be in the pub, and:

- That if he is not in the pub he did not get the job.

SUMMARY

Thinking clearly and **critically** is all-important.

Clear thinking is the ability to consider a matter objectively, ignoring everything except relevant information.

Critical thinking is the ability to come to a reasoned judgement on any matter.

It is a seven-stage process:

1. Defining the problem.
2. Formulating hypotheses and possible solutions.
3. Searching for evidence and relevant facts.
4. Making inferences and drawing logical conclusions.
5. Verifying these conclusions.
6. Making logical recommendations from these conclusions.

7. Confirming the feasibility of these recommendations.
Check, too, that you are avoiding common faults in thinking and
invalid forms of reasoning. These include:

- Selecting untypical examples;

- Describing non-existent causal relationships;

- Relying on experts;

- Exceeding the evidence;

- Presenting tautological statements;

- The fallacy of the undistributed middle;

- The fallacy of division;

- The fallacy of composition;

- The fallacy of many questions;

- The converse fallacy of accident;

- The gambler's fallacy;

- The genetic fallacy;

- The masked man fallacy; and

- Affirming the consequent or denying the antecedent.

5
Improving the Presentation of the Report

The objectives of good presentation are:

- To attract and then retain the interest of the readers;

- To help them understand the contents of the report without undue effort;

- To enable them to find their way around the report quickly; and

- To demonstrate your professionalism and, where appropriate, that of your department and/or your organisation.

In this chapter we shall consider two questions:

1. How can I improve the layout of the report?

2. How can I be sure that the typist or printer will understand my requirements?

HOW CAN I IMPROVE THE LAYOUT OF THE REPORT?

In other words, how can you make the best visual impact with your report? There are many ways of refining the appearance of the text, and a word processor can do rather better than a typewriter in this respect. Systems are being developed continually, so read your manual, or talk to the typist, to find out precisely what options are available to you.

The presentation of your report will be greatly assisted by the use of the following devices:

- Justification and centring

- Headings and subheadings

- Numbering

- Highlighting

- Variation in size and style of lettering

- Margins and spacing

- Indexing

Justification and centring

You can make the left and/or right edge of the text either beautifully aligned (justified), or ragged, as you wish. You may also want to make a piece of text centred – that is, with each line placed centrally between the right and left margins. This can be used for whole blocks of text but it is most frequently applied to headings.

Headings and subheadings

These identify and label blocks of type for the reader. It is better to structure the report with several short sections, each containing a few subheadings, than to have just a few sections, each with several subheadings or even sub-subheadings.

Once you have introduced a topic with a heading or subheading, you cannot leave that topic and move on to another one until you provide another heading or subheading. For this reason subheadings should not repeat information provided in headings. For example, if your heading is 'ABC Limited', your subheadings could be 'Production Department', 'Accounts Department' and 'Personnel Department'. There is no need to write, 'ABC Limited – Production Department'.

Headings and subheadings are not standard. You must invent them. Make sure that they:

- Are comparatively short;

- Would be expected, or at least would be easily interpreted;

- Cover all the ground (collectively);

- Do not overlap (but the same information may appear under more than one heading if it supports more than one argument);

- Are never vague (for example, avoid headings such as 'General', 'Miscellaneous' and 'Other'); and

- Are in an order which readers will find logical (perhaps in alphabetical order, in chronological order, or in order of importance).

Remember that the title of the report should be more prominent than section headings; section headings should be more prominent than paragraph headings; paragraph headings should be more prominent than subparagraph headings, and so on. Similarly, headings of the same rank should represent topics of roughly equal importance. Paradoxically, though, the less prominent the heading, the more specific and precise must be the wording below it.

Think of it this way. You are driving from London to South Wales. As you approach the motorway you see a very large sign giving fairly general directions: 'Wales and the West'. Once you have crossed the Severn Bridge you will see a slightly smaller sign giving more detailed information: 'Newport'; 'Cardiff'; 'Swansea'. As you leave the motorway at Newport you will see a smaller sign giving even more detailed information: 'The Docks'; 'Town centre'; 'Industrial Estate'. In the same way that the most prominent heading gives the general, overall subject of the report, so small subheadings may introduce quite detailed subject matter.

The choice and use of headings and subheadings also have implications for numbering systems.

Numbering
The role of numbering systems is simply to identify the various components of the report for reference and indexing purposes. There are two aspects to this:

- Numbering pages

- Numbering sections and paragraphs

You can number the pages by following one of two methods. Either simply number the pages from 1-n (n representing the final page number), beginning with the page *after* the title page. Or number the 'preliminaries' (the components *before* the main body) as (i), (ii), (iii), etc. – again beginning with the page *after* the title page, and number the remainder of the report from 1-n.

When it comes to numbering sections and paragraphs, it is very important to keep the system simple. For many writers the numbering system seems to be an end in itself; and sometimes it appears that it determines the structure of the report rather than vice versa. Here are three possible methods:

- Make the first paragraph number 1 and then number straight through to paragraph n (your final paragraph).

- Use Arabic numbering (1, 2, 3) to identify each section or heading; use letters (a, b, c) for subheadings, and use Roman numerals (i, ii, iii) for sub-subheadings. Do not go beyond three levels of numbering. If necessary re-organise the report to have more main headings.

- Use a simple two-part numbering system with headings (1, 2, 3) and subheadings (1.1, 1.2, 2.1, 2.2). Sub-paragraphs should be identified by letters or Roman numerals (a or i).

This last method is recommended. If you number **paragraphs** rather than headings or subheadings, you will avoid the complexity of three-part (1.1.1), four-part (1.1.1.1), or even five-part (1.1.1.1.1) numbering systems.

If your organisation has no standard numbering system for use in all its reports (it should have one), ask yourself what system would make things as easy as possible for your readers. Look at earlier reports. What numbering systems did they employ? Which of them worked best? Would it work equally well for this report? However, always remember that a numbering system should be determined by the structure of the report, not vice versa.

Highlighting

Sometimes it is useful to draw attention to parts of the text by methods other than headings. The major ways of doing this are by:

- Using capital rather than small letters;

- Changing the spacing either before or after;

- Indenting the words or text;

- Bulleting the words or text;

- Underlining the words or text;

- Double striking or double spacing the text;

- Using characters of different width (pitch);

- Using different typefaces, for example bold, italics (slant-ing), superscripts (raised), or subscripts (lowered).

As with any form of emphasis, it is important to be consistent and not to overdo it. The more things you emphasise, the less powerful each emphasis becomes.

Variations in size and style of lettering
A wide range of different typefaces is available for word process-ing, electronic typewriting and printing and, subject to house-rules, it is a matter of personal taste which is used, provided that:

- The typeface is clear and not too small;

- Good quality ribbons are used to produce a dark image for reproduction; and

- Printwheels are changed or typefaces cleaned when necess-ary.

Variations in the size and style of lettering will undoubtedly en-hance the presentation of the report. However again you must be consistent. For example, as we have already seen, headings and subheadings of identical size and style should always introduce subject matter of roughly equal importance. In other words, vari-ations are to be encouraged, but only where there are good reasons for them.

Margins and spacing

It is far easier for a reader to assimilate information presented in small sections than in huge, uninterrupted blocks of print. For this reason, clarity in presentation and layout is more important than economy in the use of paper. It is important to allow:

- Adequate space between the lines of print (reports are often double spaced with 1 1/2-spacing for sub-paragraphs);

- An adequate and consistent margin on the left of the page for binding;

- Clear and consistent gaps between sections and paragraphs;

- A margin of at least an inch at the top (the header zone) and bottom (the footer zone) of the page.

Thumb-index pages

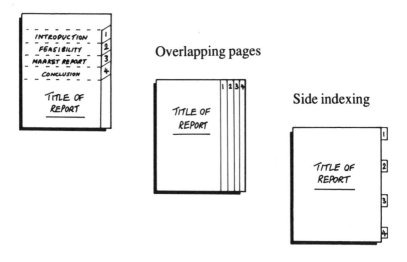

Figure 5. Indexing a report

Using indented lists of related items (such as the one on page 72) is another good way of breaking up paragraphs of text or sentences to make it easier to read. The list may be introduced by a colon, a dash, or both together (:-), and each item or phrase should be separated by a comma, a semi-colon or a full stop. The size of the indentations must be consistent.

Indexing

The report will have a contents page and it may have an index. It is possible to further improve the presentation by making it even easier for readers to find their way around the report. This can be done in a number of ways, as illustrated in Figure 5.

The thumb-index pages method is quite complex and it needs to be undertaken professionally. Therefore it is only appropriate where there will be a wide external circulation. On the other hand, the overlapping pages method is very simple: each section is identified by pages of unique width. It is most suitable for short reports. Side indexing is another straightforward method. It is achieved simply by attaching protruding selfadhesive labels to the first page of each section of the report. Each of these methods can be complemented by the use of different colour pages to identify the various sections of the report (see Chapter 9).

HOW CAN I BE SURE THAT THE TYPIST OR PRINTER WILL UNDERSTAND MY REQUIREMENTS?

It is all very well for *you* to know what you want the report to look like. But how will the typist or printer know this? The easiest way is to talk to him or her about it. If possible take a copy of a previous report produced in the style and format you require, and leave it together with your draft. Here are some 'rules' to follow when working with a typist or printer:

- Write legibly.

- Print any technical or unusual words above your cursive ('joined-up') handwriting. In this way the spelling will be clear, as will be the instruction *not* to put it in capitals.

- Double space.

- Write on one side of the page only.

- Number every page (for example, '5 of 10').

- Write 'End' in pencil at the end.

- Use a catchline to identify each sheet of the draft (for example, 'Absenteeism Report').

- Put instructions in a circle. Give full details of requirements and be clear and unambiguous.

- Observe house-rules.

- Keep a copy of everything you send to the typist/printer.

- Allow at least a fortnight for typing/printing, checking and, if necessary, correcting or re-typing/re-printing.

Careful checking and re-checking – as was stressed in Chapter 3 — are vital.

SUMMARY

The objectives of good presentation are:

- To attract and then retain the interest of the readers;

- To help them understand the contents of the report without undue effort;

- To enable them to find their way around the report quickly;

- To demonstrate your professionalism and, where appropriate, that of your department and/or your organisation.

Presentation can be greatly assisted by the use of these devices:

- Justification and centring

- Headings and subheadings

- Numbering

- Highlighting

- Variation in size and style of lettering

- Margins and spacing

- Indexing

Talk to the typist or printer, or read your typewriter or word processor instruction manual to find out what options are available to you. Then talk to them again to discuss your precise requirements. If possible leave with them a previous report which is in the same style and format that you require. Then follow the other 'rules' listed towards the end of this chapter.

Before issuing a report, always ask yourself: have its content and presentation been checked and re-checked in detail?

How to Publish a Newsletter

Graham Jones

Are you planning a community newsletter, business bulletin, house magazine, school newspaper or similar publication? With so many design and print facilities around today there has probably never been a better time to start. This practical book takes you in easy steps through the whole process. 'Good practical stuff . . . Will certainly give you a good enough understanding of the basics to cope with the normal demands of newsletter publishing.' *Writers News*. 'Until now there has been no adequate British guide . . . but that has been remedied in a new book by Graham Jones, How to Publish a Newsletter . . . a comprehensive guide to all aspects including the initial concept, design, writing, marketing, finance, contributors, advertising, editing, printing etc.' *Freelance Writing & Photography*. Graham Jones is Managing Director of ASPECT, a company which produces house magazines and other publications for client organisations.

£8.99, 176pp illus. 1 85703 045 1.

Please add postage & packing (UK £1.00 per copy. Europe £2.00 per copy. World £3.00 per copy airmail).
How To Books Ltd, Plymbridge House, Estover Road, Plymouth PL6 7PZ, United Kingdom. Tel: (0752) 695745. Fax: (0752) 695699. Telex: 45635.

6
Achieving a Good Writing Style

In Chapter 3 we took a **clinical** view of report writing (the stages of writing and the order of writing). Let's now consider the highly subjective and mentally demanding process of **effective** report writing. In other words, we shall be examining that elusive concept known as **style**.

In order to do this we shall be asking two questions:

1. What is good style?

2. How can I improve my style?

WHAT IS GOOD STYLE?

It is not possible to define precisely what good style is. Perhaps the nearest we can get to a working definition is that good style is the best way to get your message across each time you write. There are no rules. It comes down to a personal choice within the conventions of communication (see Chapter 7). However, there should always be good reasons for the style you adopt; and 'I've always written this way' is never a good reason.

The word style is not used here – as it normally is in discussing literature – as a term for appraising the quality of a writer's method of expression. A person may be well-educated and write in an excellent literary style, and yet use bad style in writing a report – because he or she fails to communicate effectively with the reader. A good style in report writing – unlike a good literary style – should combine **clarity**, **conciseness** and **directness**. It should also be 'user friendly'. Writing is sequential: one thought follows another. The **order** in which thoughts are presented must convey the meaning as much as the thoughts themselves.

A good style also should be **unobtrusive**. Think of it this way: the best sports referees are the ones you never notice. As far as possible, they allow the game to flow and they let the players take the centre stage. It is the same with good style. If the reader becomes aware of the style of writing it is probably because it is pompous, ostentatious, ambiguous, or difficult to follow. Your writing should be unobtrusive and easy to read. Allow the report to flow and let the message take the centre stage.

Finally, here are some things which certainly do *not* constitute good style:

- Humour, levity, frivolity, satire, sarcasm, irony;

- A style that is too formal, flowery, stiff or stilted;

- Colloquialisms, slang, regionalisms, vulgarisms, unnecessary contractions;

- A pompous or patronising manner.

Good report writing style is serious (concerned with important matters) without ever becoming solemn (gloomy and sombre).

HOW CAN I IMPROVE MY STYLE?

As a report writer your objective is three-fold:

- To be read,

- To be understood, and

- To be accepted.

Words are your tools of the trade, and like any other craftsperson, you should never be totally satisfied with the way you are using them. Do not assume that your style will improve with practice. Unless you work at it, it will not. There is no reason to suppose that a person who has been writing reports for twenty-five years is any better at it than a person who has been writing for just a year. Perhaps the more experienced writer has simply been regurgitating the same old report (or at least the same format and style) for the past quarter of a century, while the newer writer has been continually learning and developing his or her style.

To take another sporting analogy: junior athletes will soon improve their performance as they learn, understand and apply the fundamental techniques of their sport. This is obvious. What perhaps is less obvious is that even world champions will further improve if they are willing to accept advice from knowledgeable people and if they are able and willing to critically analyse their existing techniques, making any necessary changes to them. Indeed, this process of continual self-appraisal goes a long way to explain *why* they remain world champions. This principle applies equally to report writers.

Learning from others

So make a positive effort to improve your style. Read examples like Royal Commission Reports in your library and reports produced by other members of your organisation. Even if you are unfamiliar with the subject matter of these reports, you will soon develop a sense of when a report has succeeded and when it has failed. It is often impossible to define the precise reasons for this – it is really a gut feeling. Then read contemporary and conventional novelists: the more you read, the more your fluency will improve.

Talk to your readers. What did they think about your previous reports? What was good about them? How could they have been improved? Take their advice on board. After all, they are the important people. Be willing to learn by your mistakes and also by your successes. Paradoxically, it is often easier to accept criticism when you have been successful than when you have failed. When a football team wins 5-0, the players are elated and keen to hear how they can get even better; when it loses 5-0, they just want to go home.

Making it readable

Some reports may be difficult to write, none should be difficult to read. There are many ways to make a piece of writing readable. At the same time this will bring individuality to whatever you write. You will not only communicate more effectively; you will also give your writing extra colour and impact.

Imagine you are talking to your readers, not writing for them. They are sitting opposite you. Continually ask yourself:

Would I say that, and would I say it that way?
If the answer to either of these questions is 'No', do not write it.

Am I sure this is accurate?
Even the silliest little mistake can damage a reputation possibly built up over many years. Your credibility will be undermined or even destroyed. Accurate information is essential for effective communication.

Would they find this interesting?
It is essential for you to arouse and then maintain their interest. Otherwise they will either skim through the report or not read it at all. The film producer Samuel Goldwyn once told a writer: 'What we want is a story that starts with an earthquake and works its way up to a climax'. Keep this in mind as you draft the report. Start with some point of impact (to arouse their interest), bring in other important points approximately every 500 words (to maintain their interest), and finish on a very high point (final words are best remembered and most often acted upon).

Looking through your readers' eyes
Writing, however, is more difficult than talking; it must stand alone in conveying the message to the reader. You will have little or no opportunity, at the time the recipient reads the report, to explain, expand on, or modify what you have written. You cannot reinforce your message by non-verbal communication (gestures, facial expressions, intonations and other body language). Therefore you must try to see things as your readers will see them. Do *not* expect them to have the same mental pictures as you. Make life easy for them by being explicit.

Have you ever asked a stranger for directions? If so, you were probably bombarded with a tirade of 'lefts', 'second rights', 'next to the telephone box', 'just past the pub', and so on. Within seconds you are lost – literally. The problem is that the person giving the directions knows the area and has a mental picture of the route you should take. You do not. There is another important lesson here for the report writer. You will have spent a good deal of time on the report and you will be very familiar with its contents. By now it all seems quite obvious to you. Remember that it will *not* be at all obvious to your readers. So spell it out.

Write to *express*, not to impress. The KISS principle will help you achieve this:

- K Keep

- I It

- S Short and

- S Simple

Use short, simple and familiar words wherever possible. Always use:

- Enough words to be clear, and

- The right words to convey the precise meaning required.

However, do not use too many words. Each of them must have a purpose. The fewer words you use, the more each will do for you. Be aware of the emotional consequences of the words you use. 'Warm' words are ones which project pleasant feelings. For example, the following words might arouse these associations:

- Agree   =   Warmth

- Basic   =   Solid

- Independent   =   Freedom

- Simplicity   =   A free life

Such words are positive and their use is to be encouraged. On the other hand, 'cold' words project unpleasant feelings. For example:

- Abnormal   =   Sinister

- Afraid that   =   Gloom

- But   =   Caution

- Cannot   =   Rejection

Such words are negative and whenever possible they should be avoided.

Construct short, clear and precise sentences. It is easier to write a good short sentence than a good long one. Try not to exceed twenty words per sentence. However, an *occasional* longer sentence will vary the presentation and make the report more readable.

Make the entire report as concise as possible. Most management reports over ten pages can be shortened with considerable gain in the readers' interest, understanding and persuasiveness. However, do not confuse **conciseness** with **brevity**. A concise report is short but it contains all essential information. A brief report may have left out some important information. Continually ask yourself, "Must this information be included?". The real skill of report writing is not only knowing what to include, but also what to leave out.

When you do decide that a piece of information is essential, make sure you present it as simply as the context permits without ever over-simplifying. What makes a good television weather forecast?

1. It should be as **accurate** as possible.

2. It should be pitched at the **right level** for the kind of viewers who are likely to be watching.

A good forecaster will not say, "This is a map of Britain", or, "Low-lying nimbostatus and cumulonimbus are sailing before a west wind". The former statement is too simple and the latter is too complex and flowery for a short broadcast for the general public. Most of the viewers simply want to know whether they should take an umbrella to work tomorrow. A good forecaster will give this information and will also *gradually* introduce and explain more complex terms and information. In the same way, you will be helping nobody if you refuse to take your readers' needs and limitations into account. No writer can afford to be so self-indulgent.

Your readers will appreciate this positive approach, and they will form a higher view of you, your department, and/or your organisation. They will read subsequent reports with greater attention and enthusiasm. In time their knowledge and understanding will develop, as will your reputation. Once you have established a solid reputation you will *really* begin to guide and influence your readers.

SUMMARY

Your aims are to be read, to be understood, and to be accepted. In order to achieve this, you must always write in the most appropriate style to get your message across. A good style in report writing combines **clarity, conciseness and directness**. It should also be **unobtrusive and easy to read**. **Write to express**, not to impress, and remember the 'KISS' principle:

- K Keep

- I It

- S Short and

- S Simple

Imagine you are **talking** to your readers, not **writing** for them. Ask yourself:

- Would I say that to them?

- Would I say it that way?

- Am I sure that this is accurate?

- Will they find it interesting?

Always take your readers' needs and limitations into account.

Make a positive effort to improve your **style**. You should never be completely satisfied with it. Read contemporary and conventional novelists. Read Royal Commission Reports and reports prepared by other members of your organisation. Ask yourself why some of them succeeded while others failed. **Ask your readers** what they thought about your reports. Take their comments on board. After all, they are the important people.

7
The Use of English

This chapter will be of assistance to report writers who find some basic concepts of grammar, spelling and punctuation difficult to understand. In report writing precision and accuracy are essential. Understanding these rules will help you achieve these aims.

So let us consider two questions:

1. What basic rules of the use of English should I know?

2. What common errors in the use of English should I avoid?

WHAT BASIC RULES OF THE USE OF ENGLISH SHOULD I KNOW?

Syntax deals with the relations of words or groups of words to one another in sentences. And that is what good writing is all about: the right words in the right order. The more precise this order, the more certain that what is written will be understood. Your aim is to get your message across in a simple, straightforward and concise manner. Paradoxically, to write simply is often difficult. Here are some rules that will help you:

Rule	**Example**
Tense and Person	
1. Reports are normally written in the simple past tense. What you must decide is whether is should be in the first or third person; the first person is personal, the third is impersonal. If the report is written in the first person, you must then decide whether	First person singular: I recommend . . . First person plural: We recommend . . . Third person: It is recommended . . .

Rule	**Example**

it will be singular or plural. For internal reports the first person singular is often used. For external reports it is often the first person plural. Ask yourself how you would address the reader verbally. If it is informal, use 'I'; if it is slightly more formal, use 'We'; if it is very formal, use 'It'.

Paragraph construction

Rule	Example
1. A paragraph should read as complete in itself.	(Refer to any publication)
2. Its sentences should vary in length.	(Refer to any publication)
3. It should begin with a topic sentence.	The main reason why people want to work is to earn money.
4. The remainder of the paragraph should 'fill out' the topic sentence.	(Refer to any publication)
5. The paragraph should contain only information relevant to the topic sentence.	(Refer to any publication)
6. The final sentence should sum up that paragraph and link with the next.	While financial incentive provides strong motivation, it is not the only reason why people want to work.

Sentence construction

Rule	Example
1. A sentence is a set of words complete in itself as an expression of thought.	(Refer to any publication)
2. Generally, keep sentences as short and simple as possible. However their length and complexity should be varied to maintain interest.	Jesus wept. (John, 11:35)
3. Every sentence should have one main assertion. The normal construction is	The woman reviewed the report.

Rule	Example

subject – verb – object (or complement).

4. Words should be in a logical order.

The report will be issued next week.
not
Issuing the report will take place next week.

5. Generally, prefer the active voice to the passive voice. (But see the next five rules.)

Stephen wrote the report.
is better than
The report was written by Stephen.

6. However, if you want to say something is being done, passive is more natural.

The audit will be started next week.

7. Also, passive is better when the result is more important than the action.

The report has been typed.

8. Use the passive voice where the doer is obvious or unknown.

The office was robbed during the early hours of Monday morning.

9. The passive is also useful to avoid the continual repetition of I/we.

It was discovered that . . .

10. Use the passive voice when writing up an experiment.

A glass stopper was weighed . . .

11. The first and last words of a sentence get more attention than those in the middle.

Effective report writing requires a systematic approach, as most people appreciate.
is stronger than:
Effective report writing, as most people know, requires a systematic approach.

12. The word order can change the

She reads only on

Rule	Example
emphasis or meaning of a sentence.	Fridays. Means she does not read on any other day. She only reads on Fridays. Means she does nothing but read on Fridays.
13. Always remember the subject of the sentence.	The report highlights several weaknesses in managerial control. The situation has not improved since the last audit. *is better than*: The report highlights several weaknesses in managerial control and has not improved since the last audit. This says the report (the subject) has not improved.

Phrases and clauses

1. Avoid unnecessary phrases and clauses.	Use Obviously, *not* It is obvious that.
2. Do not overwork qualifications. A positive sentence is easier to read.	Most of the errors had been corrected but two have not been. *is better than*: While most of the errors had been corrected, two had not been.
3. Where phrases are used, they should	Stephen, who works

Rule	Example
follow the subject. A qualifying phrase can be removed without ruining the sentence.	in the accounts department, wrote the report.

Words

1. The right word, however modest, is never undignified. It will usually be concrete, familiar and exact.

   Use End
   not Terminate

2. Try to increase your vocabulary. When you meet an unfamiliar word, look it up in a dictionary. Then use it, in context.

3. Words are seldom wholly synonymous. Make sure you use the most appropriate word.

Abuse	-	Misuse
Acute	-	Chronic
Adjacent	-	Adjoining
Allocate	-	Apportion
Announce	-	Pronounce
Anticipate	-	Expect
Arbitrate	-	Mediate
Assurance	-	Insurance
Avoid	-	Evade

4. Be sparing of adjectives and adverbs.

   Investigation
   not Detailed
   investigation

5. Avoid padding words.

   Of course
   Further
   In fact

6. Never use a pronoun without considering to which noun it will appear to apply.

   Henry Cooper almost defeated Cassius Clay when he was World Champion.
   When *who* was World Champion?
   Do not rely on the knowledge of your readers.

7. Careless positioning of words is slovenly and even dangerous: it can

   The headteacher was urged to take a

Rule	**Example**
easily result in misunderstanding, confusion and even aggravation.	strong line on absenteeism by the board of governors. Did the writer really mean that?
8. Avoid tautology.	History - not Past history
9. Do not give transitional words undue emphasis. Place them inside a sentence so that they do not usurp the place of strength.	Profits were overstated. A correcting entry, however, has been made . . . *not* Profits were overstated. However, a correcting entry has been made.
10. Use the word 'a' before a word with a 'u' sound.	A European
11. Use the word 'an' before a word beginning with a silent 'h'.	An honour

Abbreviations, acronyms and jargon

1.   Your writing should be tailored to meet the needs of an identified readership. If they are *all* familiar with *all* the abbreviations, acronyms and jargon in the report, it is acceptable to leave it there. If a few people are likely to be unsure about some of it, provide a glossary or use footnotes.

2.   If you have any doubt about the use of jargon, use different and preferably simple and short words.

3.   No abbreviation should be used without giving its full form in brackets immediately after its first use.(See also *Punctuation*, rule 4)   EMS (European Monetary System)

Rule	Example

Spelling

1. There is no excuse for incorrect spelling. Poor spelling can have an adverse effect on the readers of a report which is out of all proportion to the incidence of errors. To many people, incorrect spelling indicates carelessness and lack of attention to detail. This impression must be avoided.

2. Be careful not to omit part of a word.

   Accidentally
   not Accidently

3. Be careful not to join up two words.

   In fact
   not Infact

4. 'I' before 'e', except after 'c'.

   Field, yield, receive
   However, be wary of some weird exceptions: Neither, either, leisure

5. The prefix 'dis' is not hyphenated.

   Discontinue
   not Dis-continue

6. The prefix 'sub' is not usually hyphenated.

   Subeditor
   not sub-editor

7. The prefix 'un' is normally not hyphenated.

   Uncertified
   not Un-certified

8. To form the plural of words ending in 'y':

   If there is a consonant immediately before the 'y' in the singular, then the plural is 'ies'.

   Lady - Ladies

   If there is a vowel immediately before the 'y' in the singular, then the plural is 'ys'.

   Valley - Valleys

9. Pay particular attention to words which are pronounced the same, or very similarly, but are spelt differently.

   There and their
   To, too and two

Rule	**Example**

Punctuation

1. The purpose of punctuation is simply to make it easier for the reader to understand the text.

2. A good way to check your punctuation is to read aloud. Whenever you pause or change the inflexion in your voice, you should have some form of punctuation mark.

3. Use a capital letter to start the first word of a sentence. Also use them for people's names, place names and titles. Many report writers also use capitals for indexes and section headings. Problems occur in headings which are a mixture of capitals and lower case letters, but the basic rule is to use capitals for the first letter of each word which is not either a preposition or a conjunction.

   John Smith; London; Lord High Chancellor; Department of Energy; 'Absenteeism at ABC Limited, 1990-94'.

4. Use a full stop (.) to end a sentence. Also use them after each letter which represents a word in an abbreviation.

   E.F.C., European Forestry Commission (three words). Nat. Hist., Natural History (two words). km., kilometre (one word).

5. Use a comma (,) to separate three or more items.

   We consider glass, plastic, polythene and polystyrene.

6. Use a comma to represent a pause in a sentence.

   The report, which was written by Stephen, will be issued next week.

7. Use a comma to differentiate between clauses that define and those that comment.

   Mr Jones who was elected chairman takes over from Mr Smith on Tuesday.

Rule	Example
	(definition) Mr Jones, who was elected chairman takes over from Mr Smith on Tuesday. (comment)
8. Use a semi-colon (;) instead of a full stop to join 'sentences' which have some bearing on each other.	England won the World Cup in 1966; Geoff Hurst scored three goals in the final.
9. Use a semi-colon to mark off phrases (especially lists) in which a comma already appears.	The men worked in fields; the women, in the factory; the children, in the school.
10. Use a colon (:) to represent 'that is to say' or 'namely'.	There are many sources of inform-ation: people, places, events, publications, information techno-logy and the media.
11. Use a colon to introduce an explanatory statement.	This is our decision: to accept the offer and sell the factory.
12. Use a colon to introduce a quotation where a comma already appears in the sentence.	Referring to her notes, she said: 'I visited the office on 16 September'.
13. Uses dashes (–) instead of brackets to indicate parenthesis. Dashes are stronger than a pair of commas but weaker than brackets.	The athletes – there were ten of them – all completed the race.
14. Use a dash to indicate an additional thought.	Brown came to this month's meeting – it was the first he had attended since April.
15. Use a dash where a word is repeated, together with an explanation or with	We need to win the match today – and

Rule	Example
	elaboration.	to win it by at least three goals.

16. Use an apostrophe (') to shorten a word. Place it above the space created by the removal of the letter. Such contractions are not usual in formal writing.

is not   – isn't
do not – don't

17. Use apostrophes to indicate possession. If the word requiring the apostrophe is singular, place it before the 's'; if it is plural, place it after the 's'.

Britain's voters (the voters of Britain). Teachers' unions (unions of teachers).

18. Do not use apostrophes with possessive pronouns or where they are otherwise not required.

Hers *not* her's
Giros *not* giro's

19. Use inverted commas ("...") immediately before and after a direct quotation.

As Wellington said, ''publish and be damned''.

20. Use double and single inverted commas where there is a quotation within a quotation.

He said: ''As Ford remarked, 'you can have any colour so long as it's black.'''

21. Use inverted commas where a word is used 'oddly'.

A semi-colon can be used to join 'sentences' together. Inverted commas are used because they are no longer separate sentences.

22. Do not use inverted commas when stating facts.

Everest is the highest mountain in the world. This statement does not require inverted commas.

23. Use a question mark (?) at the end of a sentence containing a query.

That is quite straight-forward, isn't it?

24. Use an explanation mark (!) to suggest a sudden change of emotion.

You must be joking!

Rule	Example

Use them sparingly.
25. Use brackets ( ) to enclose explanatory words.

Report writers must be aware of the main principles of law of libel (defamation published in a permanent form).

Good English is not written by accident. Read it through and see if it sounds grammatical. If it does not, amend it until it does. If necessary, throw it away and start again.

WHAT COMMON ERRORS IN THE USE OF ENGLISH SHOULD I AVOID?

By way of a little light relief, here are twenty statements, each of which is itself a demonstration of the fault it describes:

- First and foremost, avoid clichés like the plague.

- A verb have to agree with its subject.

- There is no excuse for incorrect spelling.

- Avoid abstract nouns, in truth they are not readily understood.

- Never use no double negatives.

- It makes sense not to use the same words in two senses in the same sentence.

- Avoid run-on sentences they are hard to read.

- Place pronouns as close as possible, especially in long sentences, to their antecedents.

- ''Avoid overuse of 'quotation marks'''.

- Avoid all un-necessary hyphens.

- Use commas only, when necessary.

- Do not overuse exclamation marks!!!

- Don't use contractions in formal writing.

- Always avoid all awkward and affected alliteration.

- Avoid using the same words over and over and over again.

- Verily it is incumbent upon you to avoid ensamples of archaic words.

- Avoid mixed metaphors; with enough time on your hands you should never end up with egg on your face.

- Having drafted the report, all dangling principles must be deleted.

- Make sure you never a word out.

- *Le mot de la fin:* do not use foreign words or phrases if there are good English equivalent words or phrases.

SUMMARY

Writers often look at what they have written and have an uneasy feeling that it is not quite right, but they do not know why. Understanding the basic concepts of grammar, spelling and punctuation helps identify the malady and its root cause. The cure then presents itself. An understanding of the key rules of the use of English, and an examination of some examples of their violation, will help to improve your writing.

8
Using Illustrations

Well produced and *appropriate* illustrations really enhance a report. They make the information readily understandable, easily digestible and memorable. It is much easier to assimilate information presented pictorially.

In this chapter we shall consider these two questions:

1. When, where and how should I include illustrations?

2. What kinds of illustration should I include?

WHEN, WHERE AND HOW SHOULD I INCLUDE ILLUSTRATIONS?

Illustrations are useful only when they are easier to understand than the words or figures they represent. They must be relevant to the text, and they should never be included for their own sake.

An illustration is a pictorial representation of information. Figure 1, for example, is an algorithm which will help you to decide whether any particular illustration would really add anything useful to your report. Ask yourself the 'so what?' question: does every illustration have something to say within the overall context of the report? If there is no meaningful answer to 'so what?', then the illustration is worthless. If you have a positive answer to the question, then the illustration should be included. The algorithm will also help you to decide where it should be placed. Ask yourself whether it would break the flow of the report or distract the reader. If the answer is 'no', place it in the main body of the report, as close to the point of reference as possible. If the answer is 'yes', put it in an appendix.

Another good way to help you decide the placing of an illustration is to ask yourself whether it is **fundamental** to the arguments in the text or merely **supplementary** to them. If the reader *needs* to see an illustration in order to understand the text – or if it is referred to several times – it must be placed within the main body of the report. If the reader does not need to see it, it may be preferable to place it in an appendix – especially if there are several other illustrations.

When you use an illustration bear these points in mind:

- Give it a caption and figure number.

- Where appropriate, acknowledge your source.

- Keep it simple; do not include too much detail.

- Use a sensible scale and give details of this scale.

- Discuss and explain its significance.

- Make sure it proves what you intended it to prove.

- Do not overdo it; too many illustrations will overwhelm the reader.

- If there are more than just one or two illustrations, list them on the contents page.

As you continue to read this book, you will find that I have broken the second of these 'rules'; I have not acknowledged the source below each illustration. The reason for this is simple. This book is really a report on effective report writing. As the writer, it is my responsibility always to consider the requirements of the readers (you). My common sense tells me that you are more interested to know that Figure 6 is an example of a pie chart rather than knowing that it shows advertising expenditure in 1993, broken down by main media category, or that the source of this data was *The Advertising Statistics Yearbook*. As with all aspects of report writing, when common sense and a 'rule' come into conflict, common sense must prevail.

WHAT KINDS OF ILLUSTRATION SHOULD I INCLUDE?

As always, remember your readers. Your aim is to include illustrations which arouse their interest and help them to a quicker understanding.

Never try to be clever. Just use clear, simple, uncluttered and appropriate illustrations. Concentrate on essentials. There are several templates and stencils on the market which will help your presentation.

Ask yourself: What is the **purpose** of the illustration? Let's consider three of the most common answers to this question:

- To give a general impression;

- To show detailed information; or

- To show the structure and working of a system.

Illustrations which give a general impression
Three of the best ways of illustrating this are by the use of a:

- Pie chart

- Bar chart or

- Pictogram

Pie charts
A pie chart is a circle divided by radii into sectors whose areas are proportional to the relative magnitudes or frequencies of a set of items. It is an excellent method of illustrating such **relative proportions**.

Here's an example. In 1993 total advertising expenditure in the UK was as follows:

Press	:	£4,816 million
Television	:	£2,303 million
Poster and Transport	:	£267 million
Radio	:	£149 million
Cinema	:	£42 million

Suppose you wish to illustrate these figures by means of a pie chart. To calculate the number of degrees appropriate to each sector, use this equation:

$$\frac{\text{Sector total} \quad \text{x} \quad 360°}{\text{Total population}}$$

For example, the calculation for the press is:

$$\frac{4816 \times 360°}{7577} = 228.8°$$

Three variations on the basic pie chart are the:

- Illustrated pie chart
- Half-pie chart
- Multi-pie chart

The **illustrated pie chart** simply includes some illustration or drawing relevant to the topic. In the example given in Figure 6, it probably would be a few newspapers, a television set, and so on.

The **half-pie chart** depicts only the top half of a circle. To calculate the number of degrees appropriate to each division, multiply by 180° instead of 360°.

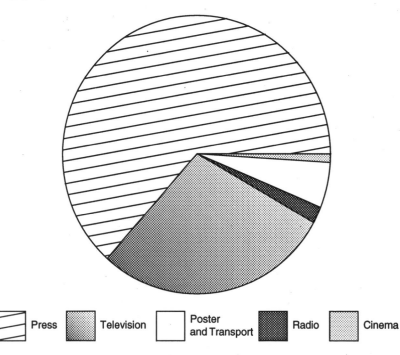

Figure 6. A pie chart

The **multi-pie chart** consists of two or more pie charts each with similar constituent parts.

The size of each pie chart will depend on its relative importance. For example, a pie chart illustrating the distribution of trade in the USA would be larger than one for Britain. These charts are quite difficult to draw.

Bar charts
This is a simple way of comparing values by using bars of various lengths, drawn to scale. In other words, it is an excellent way of illustrating **relationships** between items. Figure 7 is a bar chart showing the main crops grown in Britain during 1993 (source: *Annual Review of Agriculture*).

Variations on the basic bar chart include the:

- Sectional bar chart
- Percentage bar chart
- Dual bar chart

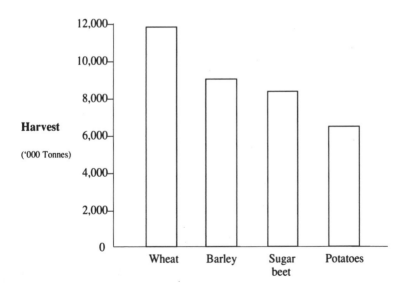

Figure 7. A bar chart

Sectional bar charts show the magnitude of items *and* their constituent parts. For example, a chart showing passenger traffic at Britain's four main airports in 1980, 1985 and 1990 would comprise three bars (showing the total traffic for the three years), each divided into four (showing the traffic going through the individual airports).

Percentage bar charts show the percentage a constituent part bears to the whole. For example, if you wanted to compare the number of votes cast for political parties at the last general election with the number of candidates elected, you would show two bars of identical size; one divided to reflect the percentage of total votes cast for each party, the other the percentage of total MPs elected.

Dual bar charts compare two or more related quantities over time. For example, they could show the percentage of households with cars, central heating and telephones in 1985 and 1990. For each of these there would be two bars, next to each other, one for 1985 and one for 1990.

Pictogram
This is similar to a bar chart except that it is usually horizontal and it uses symbols instead of bars to represent magnitudes or frequencies. Figure 8 is a pictogram which shows the passenger traffic at Britain's main airports in 1990 (source: *Transport Statistics, Great Britain*).

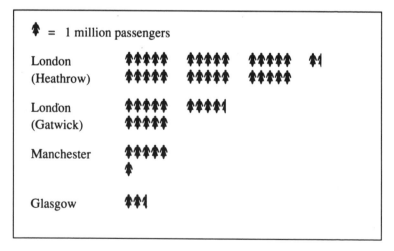

Figure 8. A pictogram

Illustrations which show detailed information

These illustrations must facilitate detailed readings or provide detailed answers to questions. Three of the most effective ways of achieving these aims are by the use of a:

- Graph
- Algorithm or
- Table

Graph

A graph shows the relationship between two variables, and it is an excellent method of illustrating detailed relationships between items. The **vertical axis** is usually scaled in units of the dependent variable (the quantity which is being controlled or adjusted), while the **horizontal axis** is usually scaled in units of the independent variable (the quantity being observed).

A variation on the **simple graph** is the pictorial line graph where 'pictures' are added. For example, if you were comparing the efficiency of postal services in different parts of the world, you could superimpose national stamps to distinguish the countries represented by the various lines on the graph. However, be careful not to make any graph too complex. There are also several other types of graph, each associated with one or more professions. For example, a financial or management accountant would be interested in break-even charts, investment risk profiles, sensitivity analyses, and so on.

Here are some rules to follow when drawing graphs:

- When undertaking experimental work, draw a rough graph as you record your results. In this way you can check any irregularities immediately.
- Choose a scale in which the lines or the curve will occupy most of the graph.
- If possible the graph should be arranged so that it reads the same way up as the text.
- In most experimental work, lines should form smooth curves.
- Where results do not follow a smooth curve, or where the graph does not represent experimental findings (perhaps it shows sales results), points should be joined by straight lines. Where this occurs you *cannot* read off between the points as with a curve.

Algorithm
An algorithm is a flow chart which will answer a question, or solve
a problem, or undertake a procedure, within a finite number of
steps. It does this by considering only those factors that are relevant
to the question, problem or procedure. Algorithms are often difficult to write but, once prepared, they are excellent illustrations,
particularly for instructional manuals. For example, they can be
used to describe fault finding procedures, or how to carry out
complicated checks on machinery. They can be used by readers
with no knowledge of operational theory. In Chapter 1 (Figure 1),
there is a very simple algorithm to help the report writer decide
whether to include a particular piece of information in the report
and, if so, where to place it.

Table
Strictly speaking, a table is not an illustration or a pictorial
representation. However, it is included here because neither is it
part of the text of the report. Your aim is to make the report as
readable as possible and the use of a table is often the best way
of achieving this aim while also presenting some essential,
detailed information.

A common mistake in writing reports is to produce too many
figures and too few explanations. The principles to follow are
three-fold:

- Always check figures very carefully before including them;
- Restrict figures to those which are meaningful; and
- Make sure they are consistently produced and interpreted.

However, in some reports it is essential to include a large number
of highly detailed findings. The strength of these reports is often
based almost entirely on their factual content. In such cases it is
usually best to use **appendixes**. Where appropriate, it is perfectly
acceptable for your appendixes to be longer than all the rest of the
report. But think of your readers. How are they likely to read the
report? They will probably read the preliminaries and then the
main body. The appendixes may well be an afterthought. So
highlight any particularly significant findings in these preliminaries and in the main body. If you find it necessary to refer to
certain tables on several occasions, it is better to include them in
the main body.

Here are some rules when compiling statistical tables:

- Avoid tables where there are over ten columns.

- Label each column and row to identify the data.

- If a column shows amounts, state the units.

- If columns are too long, double space after every fifth entry.

- If a particular column or row lacks data, use dashes in each space lacking the data.

- If they improve legibility, use vertical lines to separate columns.

- Do not mix decimals (29.3) with fractions ($17^1/_2$).

Never assume that your readers will draw the right conclusion from the figures. They may quite easily not be reading them at all; or they may read them and come to the wrong conclusions, or perhaps no conclusions. Always say **in words** what they mean.

Illustrations which show the structure and working of a system

Here the word **system** is used in its widest sense to include any structure or process composed of interrelated, interdependent, or interacting elements forming a collective entity. The management structure of a company is a system. So is a clerical or production process. So is the way a piece of machinery is built, and is used.

Three of the best ways of illustrating the structure and working of a system are by the use of a:

- Chart

- Diagram or

- Photograph

Chart
We have already considered pie charts, bar charts and graphs.

Other charts of potential value to report writers include:

- Flow charts

- Organisational charts

- Maps and plans

- Systematic diagrams

A **flow chart** is a diagrammatic representation of the sequence of operations or equipment in a natural, industrial or organisational process. It is commonly used to describe industrial and clerical processes, and computer systems and programs. Figure 9 is a flow chart illustrating inventory control by means of the calculation of the value of the inventory. As you will see, a flow chart uses a standard set of symbols. In this instance the symbols are those associated with computer science.

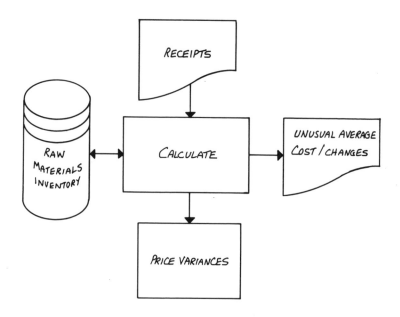

Figure 9. A flow chart

An **organisational chart** depicts the hierarchy of, and the lines of command within, an organisation. Figure 10 represents a simple organisation which could well exist within the transport services function of a small manufacturing company.

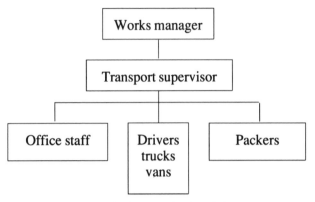

Figure 10. An organisational chart

When **maps** or **plans** are included in a report it is important to state whether or not they are completely to scale. Always include a small arrow pointing northwards.

Systematic diagrams are useful when you wish to illustrate what connects with what. They are commonly used for wiring diagrams and transport connections. The famous map of the London Underground is an example of a systematic diagram.

Diagram
This is a drawing or sketch which demonstrates the form or working of something. There are several types of diagram, including:

- Orthographic drawing
- Isometric drawing
- Perspective drawing
- Exploded drawing
- Cut-away drawing

An **orthographic drawing** is composed of the plans of the back, front and side elevations of an object. It must be drawn to scale. While it is very useful for designers and manufacturers, it is of little value for anyone who wants to know what it actually looks like.

An **isometric drawing** provides a pictorial method of illustrating something. Three faces are shown at once but no allowance is made for perspective; all the lines that are parallel on the object are drawn parallel. It is easy to draw but the lack of perspective makes it look peculiar, as can be seen in Figure 11.

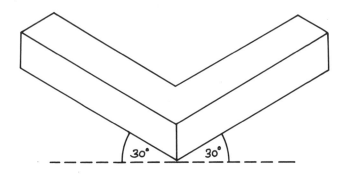

Figure 11. An isometric drawing

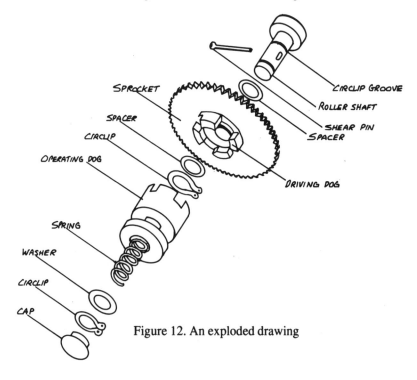

Figure 12. An exploded drawing

A **perspective drawing**, on the other hand, shows an object as it is seen by the human eye. It is more difficult to draw but it looks more natural.

An **exploded drawing** provides a pictorial representation of how something is constructed. It does this by showing its components in assembly as though they were spread out along an invisible axis. Figure 12 is an exploded drawing of a lawn mower dog clutch.

A **cut-away drawing** shows an object with its 'cover off' in certain places, or with a slice removed to reveal the inside. Figure 13 is a cut-away drawing of an electric bell.

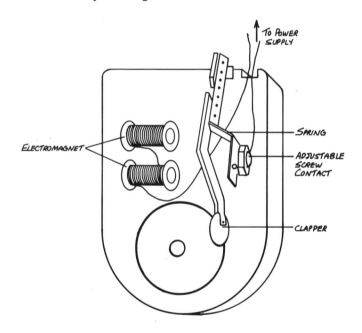

Figure 13. A cut-away drawing

In general, a line drawing is better for technical illustrations than a photograph since it can be shaded or highlighted to emphasise essential points. It also reproduces well. However, a report writer should also consider whether the inclusion of a photograph would be useful and justifiable.

Photograph
A *good* photograph will show the exact appearance of an object or

a situation at a particular moment in time. It is therefore useful for showing newly created objects, ones never seen before, ones at the end of a particular stage of development, or ones worn out or damaged. If you need to show the size of an object, it is a good idea to include some familiar object in the photograph – perhaps a hand, a finger, a coin, a matchbox, or a ruler.

Unless you are already a very competent photographer, it is best to keep things as simple as possible. Use an automatic 35mm SLR (Single Lens Reflex) camera. You will see exactly what passes onto the film; you will achieve an accurate focus; you will be using a system of lenses and accessories which will allow an enormous variety and flexibility of output, and you can expect good results in a variety of lighting conditions.

However, **things do go wrong** – especially if you are not an experienced photographer. For this reason also use a back up Polaroid camera. You will be able to see your results within seconds. If you are not satisfied with them, keep clicking away until you are.

Photographs are expensive unless there is a very limited report circulation. Ask yourself whether it is really necessary to produce multiple prints to affix to each copy. Will half-tones be adequate? The answer to this question will depend largely on the number of copies and the nature of the readership. You will have seen property descriptions prepared by estate agents. On the description of an imposing property (that is, an expensive one likely to be of interest to rich people), you will probably see a print. On the description of a less imposing property (that is, a cheaper one likely to be of interest to people of more moderate means), you will probably see a half-tone. So ask yourself what you are trying to 'sell' and to whom you are trying to sell it.

In this chapter we have looked at some of the most common methods of illustrating reports. If you want to find out more about them or if you wish to consider some other possibilities, refer to *Learn to Draw Charts and Diagrams Step by Step* by Bruce Robertson (see Further Reading, p. 153).

SUMMARY

- Well produced and *appropriate* illustrations really enhance a report. They make information readily understandable, easily digestible and memorable. It is much easier to assimilate information presented pictorially.

- However, illustrations should only be used if they are easier to understand than the words or figures they represent. They should *never* be included for their own sake. Ask yourself: are they relevant to the text?

- Before you decide the kind of illustration you will use, ask yourself what is its *purpose*: is it intended to give an overall impression of something, to show some detailed findings, or to show the structure and working of a system? Then choose the most appropriate illustration to achieve this end.

- If a reader will *need* to see the illustration in order to understand the text, place it as close to the point of reference as possible. However if it is merely *supplementary* to the text, it is often preferable to place it in an appendix.

9
The Choice of Paper, Covers and Binding

Finally, a word about the choice of paper, covers and binding for your report. Appearance really does matter. So does durability. It is obvious that glossy, professional-looking reports will project the sort of image that most companies wish to foster with existing and potential customers and/or shareholders. Perhaps what is less obvious is that sometimes it is desirable to produce low-budget reports for more than just reasons of economy. For example, it is rarely necessary to produce an ornate product if it is for internal consumption only. Even if your department does have money to burn, it is not a good idea to advertise the fact.

As you think about the physical construction and appearance of a report, bear these points in mind:

- Your purpose (the **action** you intend the report to generate);

- The readership (number and nature);

- The expected life of the report (including the number of likely references to be made to it);

- What materials and facilities are available within your organisation; and

- The cost of these various options (and your budget).

In this chapter we shall be answering two straightforward questions:

1. What kind of paper should I use?

2. What covers and binding should I use?

WHAT KIND OF PAPER SHOULD I USE?

There are three aspects to this question:

- Size

- Quality

- Colour

Most reports are written on **A4 size paper** (297 x 210 mm). The **quality of paper** you choose will depend on all the factors listed above. For example, do not use poor quality paper if the report is likely to be referred to frequently.

The importance of **conciseness** has been stressed throughout this book (Keep It Short and Simple). However, this does not mean use as little paper as possible. As you saw in Chapter 5, it is also important not to present the reader with huge blocks of uninterrupted type. If you are really concerned about the future of the Scandinavian and Canadian forests, the amount of paper saved at the planning stage (Chapter 1) will more than compensate for an extra few sheets in the report itself. You could also think about using re-cycled paper.

It is customary for reports to be written on white paper. However sometimes it is useful to use different **colour paper** in different sections of the report. If you do this be sure that:

- The colours are easily distinguishable;

- Dark colours are avoided; and

- The different sections are logical and rational.

Alternatively, you could use white paper throughout and coloured partitions between the sections.

WHAT COVERS AND BINDING SHOULD I USE?

Covers

Every report should have covers, if only an extra sheet of paper at the back and front to serve as a dust jacket. However most reports will be enclosed by glossy boards (cards). Other covers will be made of plastic or even imitation leather, perhaps with a pocket so that other related documents can be kept with the report.

Many reports will have no more than a title on their covers. Others will include the organisation's name and logo and/or a space for a reference number, the date of issue and the name of the department responsible for the production of the report. Sometimes a 'window' will have been cut out of the front cover. This allows the reader to see the title as it appears on the title page.

Think carefully about the colour of your covers. Dark ones are often very depressing while very light ones or ones using a combination of bright colours may give an unwanted impression of light-heartedness. 'Safe' colours for reports are either blue or green.

Binding

There are several inexpensive binding systems available. Your choice will depend largely upon:

- The size of the report;

- Whether amendments will be necessary;

- Whether inserts will be necessary;

- The distribution requirements;

- The quality requirements;

- The binding methods used for other related reports; and

- What system or systems are available within your organisation.

Here are some common methods of binding:

- Treasury tag
- Stapling
- Plastic gripper
- Gluing
- Stitching
- Ring binding

Treasury tag
Tags come in various sizes identified by their colour. Punch a hole in the top left of the report. Make sure it is at least an inch into the paper both from the top and the left, otherwise sheets will soon become detached. For larger reports, also punch a hole at the bottom left, or use a four-hole punch. This method of binding is suitable where amendments will be likely and/or where inserts such as maps and plans are expected. Do not use tags to bind reports which are larger than 100 sheets.

Stapling
Here you simply staple the covers and pages at the top left corner. For reports of 10 to 20 pages, it is best to staple them from the front and the back. Then place the report in a plastic wallet. A more sophisticated method is to staple down the left hand side and cover them with adhesive binding strip. Be sure to leave wide margins, and double staple at the top and bottom of the report. Never use paper clips. Pins are slightly better, but for reasons of safety they are not recommended.

Plastic gripper
This method is an improvement on the use of staples down the left side of the report, but the principle is the same. Use a plastic slide-grip along the left hand edge of the assembled covers and sheets. Once again, remember to leave wide margins if you intend to use this system.

Gluing
The edges of the sheets are glued and fixed into the spine of a fabric, card or plastic cover. This method is suitable only for reports of about 25 pages or more and it should be attempted only by the most dexterous of report writers. A more sophisticated method is known as hot metal gluing.

Stitching
Here the report is made up of sheets folded in the middle to make two single-sided or four double-sided pages. They are then bound by a method known as saddle stitching. This system is not suitable for larger reports because the pages tend to become distorted. It is possible to have reports stitched and cased commercially in hard-back form. However, this would be a far more expensive exercise.

Ring binding

This gives a report a professional appearance and it is suitable for works of up to around 20 sheets. You will need to have access to a special machine which perforates the binding edge and then threads the binding (plastic or wire) through the holes in the covers and the report. The pages of the report will then lie flat when opened. Plastic binding is preferred because sheets can be added or removed, as required. This is not possible with wire binding. Any organisation which produces reports regularly and/or in quantity should seriously consider acquiring a ring binding machine.

SUMMARY

Appearance and durability matter. Your choice of paper, covers and binding will be strongly influenced by your purpose, your readership, the expected life of your report, the options available to you within your organisation, and their costs.

Paper

Most reports are written on A4 size white paper. However, sometimes it is useful to use different colours to identify the various sections of a report.

Covers

Every report should have covers. These are usually glossy cards which may include no more than the title. 'Safe' colours for covers are blue or green.

Binding

There are many inexpensive methods of binding a report. Choose the one most suitable for your report, bearing in mind:

- The size of the report;
- Whether any amendments and/or inserts will be necessary;
- The distribution and quality requirements;
- The binding methods used for other related reports; and
- What systems are available within your organisation, and what their relative costs are.

10
Some Common Types
of Report

- Accident reports

- Agendas for committee meetings

- Annual reports

- Appraisal reports

- Audit reports

- Comparative testing reports

- Duty notes reports

- Explanatory reports

- Feasibility reports

- Informative reports

- Instructional manuals

- Interview reports

- Investigation into financial affairs of a company reports

- Minutes

- Process description reports

- Progress reports

- Research reports

- Scientific reports

- Student project reports

- Systems evaluation reports

- Technical reports

- Technological reports

- Trouble-shooting reports

This chapter considers some of the most common types of report which you may be required to produce. They cover different subjects, and they have different purposes and readerships. For this reason they have different structures; they are made up of a variety of combinations of report components (introductions, summaries, and so on), and these components are often given different names in different types of report. Every report should have a title page.

In Chapter 1 we discussed report components in some detail. The comments here are intended to complement that discussion by pointing out the **particular emphases** associated with each report type. We shall do this by answering two questions:

1. What points should I bear in mind?

2. What would be a suitable format?

Use this information and advice to help you decide the most appropriate style, format and contents for your report. However, use them **flexibly**; you must also bear in mind:

- The requirements of the person who commissioned the report;
- House-style;
- Custom and conventions;
- Your objective(s);
- Your readership; and
- Common sense.

As you plan and later draft your report, remember that while every report should be different, every report also should have some similarities. It must present relevant facts accurately and in a way that is both acceptable and intelligible to its readers. In other words, it must have a beginning, a middle and an end. Only then can you expect to achieve these three essential aims:

- to be read without unnecessary delay,
- to be understood without undue effort, and
- to be accepted.

So always think about the needs of your readers. They are the important people, and they have a right to expect you to make things as easy for them as possible. If you do not help them, why should they help you?

ACCIDENT REPORTS

These reports hopefully will not be required on a regular basis.

What points should I bear in mind?
Balance speed with accuracy. The reason for speed is so that all salient facts are accurately recorded before details are forgotten. The reasons for accuracy are to minimise the risk of any possible recurrence, to comply with the law and to be prepared to face a possible claim for damages. You will require accurate illustrations supplemented by statements from participants, witnesses and experts.

What would be a suitable format?
If you have no formal report form, use these headings:

1. What was the accident?
2. Where and when did it occur?
3. Who was involved?
4. Was any injury sustained? If so, what was it?
5. Who reported the accident?
6. What medical treatment was applied – when and by whom?
7. What caused the accident?
8. What has been done to correct the trouble?
9. What recommendations do you have to avoid a recurrence?

AGENDAS FOR COMMITTEE MEETINGS

An agenda is a list of items to be discussed during a meeting. It *must* be drawn up in advance.

What points should I bear in mind?

An agenda may take various forms, according to the requirements and, in some cases, the kind of meeting to which it refers. Be sure you know precisely what is expected of you. Here are two common forms of committee agenda:

- the standard agenda

- the discussive agenda

The standard agenda simply lists the subjects to be discussed, and the order in which they will be taken.

The discussive agenda is designed to stimulate thought *before* and comment *at* the meeting. It is often used for 'one-off' meetings.

No business should be placed on an agenda unless it comes within the scope of the committee, and it is within the power of the committee to deal with it. Conversely, no relevant item of business should be omitted.

In deciding what to include on an agenda, bear these points in mind:

- Talk to the chairperson and other committee members who may have business to include.

- Refer to the minutes of previous meetings for any business or discussions which were then deferred, and for reminders of routine annual, half-yearly, quarterly or monthly recurring items.

- Keep a special file of documents which are likely to be required at the next meeting. Sort and arrange them before drafting the agenda.

Then think carefully about the order in which items should come up for discussion. Consider these factors when deciding the order:

- Refer to any rules governing the meeting which regulate the order in which items of business are dealt with.

- If there are no such rules, make sure the items are in a logical order. Wherever possible, the end of the discussion on one item should lead naturally on to the next.

- It is normally preferable to put routine business first.

- Try to place difficult or contentious items just after half-way through the agenda, with some simple, uncontentious items before and after them. This is known as a bell-curve structure. Begin with some items likely to achieve a consensus. Then move on to your more 'difficult' subjects. Conclude with more simple, uncontentious items so that the meeting will end amicably.

Make it easy for the committee members to find their way through the agenda by using these devices:

- Number all items consecutively, beginning with '1'.
- If separate documents are required for any item, quote the reference number under the appropriate heading together with the date of circulation. If they are to be circulated later, or handed out at the meeting, say so.
- Where an item on the agenda is being continued or carried forward from a previous meeting, quote the minute and date of that meeting.
- At the end of the agenda provide a checklist of the documents required for the meeting, in the order in which they will be needed.

Finally, obtain the chairperson's approval of the agenda *before* circulating it. This agenda will form the basis of the minutes of the meeting (see below).

What would be a suitable format?
Standard agenda
A suitable format for a standard agenda would be as follows:

1. Heading (including where and when the meeting will take place)

2.   Apologies for Absence

3.   Minutes of the Previous meeting

4.

5.
        } Items requiring the attention of the committee
6.

7.

8.   Any Other Business ('leftovers', *not* items that should have been discussed within section 4-7)

9.   Date of Next Meeting (also give the time and location)

10.   Papers Required for the Meeting (in the order that they will be needed).

Items 1-3 and 8-10 are standard. Between them come all other items requiring the attention of the committee.

Discussive agenda
A discussive agenda could be structured as follows:

1.   Heading (including where and when the meeting will take place)

2.   Introduction (what will be discussed, and why – keep it fairly general)

3.   Scope (what are the boundaries of the discussion?)

4.   Discussion points (list the items to be discussed and the reasons for discussing them)

5.   Possible action (what options are open to the committee?)

6.   Summary (the reason for the meeting; what it hopes to achieve and why members should attend and contribute)

7.   Papers required for the meeting (in the order that they will be needed).

ANNUAL REPORTS

An annual report lists the achievements and failures of an organisation. It is a progress report in which every department is accounted for.

What points should I bear in mind?

The physical appearance of annual reports is crucial. For that reason they are usually prepared professionally. The cover and the first few pages must attract and then maintain the readers' interest. Make the cover attractive and eye-catching; keep the text well spaced and content not too heavy. Begin with some simple facts about the organisation and what it does. Use short paragraphs with bold print to emphasise the key points. Include illustrations to attract interest and to break up overbearing columns of figures. When you use photographs of people, record their names. Too many reports give the name of their chairperson but then describe a member of staff as 'an engineer', or whatever. Workers, like chairpersons, have names.

As a general rule, the shorter the report the better the chances of attracting a fringe readership. So make sure you gather *relevant* data from all parts of your organisation. Obviously every department will wish to emphasise its successes and gloss over (or simply ignore) its failures. For this reason the use of standard questionnaires is recommended. This will provide only the information you require, and it will be in a uniform format and style. Use this as the basis of the main body of the report.

Annual reports usually include a chairperson's statement. Most of these statements are far too long. Tactfully explain that all that is required is a résumé and critical analysis of the past year's work, and an assessment of prospects. This section should pass logically from topic to topic. It should be informative, businesslike and balanced. It should also be concise – no more than 1,000 words (less if possible).

What would be a suitable format?

This depends on the nature of the organisation and the readership. Here is one possible format:

- Contents list

- What the organisation does

- Some of the year's highlights

- Chairperson's Statement

- Main body (possibly department to department, or task to task)

- Accounts

- Appendixes

A standard format is useful for year-to-year comparisons.

APPRAISAL REPORTS

These appraise a person's performance on his or her current job, identify methods of improving this performance, highlight training needs, and often assess suitability for another job, promotion, and/or a change in salary.

What points should I bear in mind?
Appraisal reports are very important because what you write will have a direct effect on people's career prospects. They are very difficult to write. The dilemma is that, on the one hand, you need to know a person quite well in order to write a fair report while, on the other hand, it can be difficult to be objective when you know a person quite well. Not only that, you will need to decide what is relevant and what is not. For example behavioural patterns are likely to change according to circumstances, and we tend to remember extremes of behaviour. Ask yourself: 'Are they really typical?' Try keeping a notebook and update it regularly in order to build up an *accurate* and *balanced* picture of people. Also talk with them about this throughout the year, not just at counselling and appraisal interviews.

The responsibilities of an appraisal report writer, therefore, are acute. Be specific and avoid euphemisms. You must be able to justify every tick in the matrix boxes, and every word and phrase you use.

What would be a suitable format?
You may be required to complete a standard form. Details will vary from organisation to organisation, but the broad outline of an

appraisal report should cover the following headings and questions:

1. The Job

- The job description, its objectives, component tasks, methods and resources.

- Are they satisfactory?

- If not, why not?

- What changes are required?

- What action is recommended – by whom, how and why?

2. Job Performance

- What objectives must be met and what tasks must be fulfilled?

- Have these been achieved?

- What is the actual evidence from work performance, indicating success or failure?

- How far have any failures been within or outside the job-holder's control?

- What does the evidence of past performance show about the strengths and weaknesses in knowledge, skills and attitudes of the job-holder?

- What precise action is recommended – by whom, how and when – to build on strengths, to remedy weaknesses and to develop the individual by means of training and further work experience?

3. Summary of Action Proposed

- What action has been agreed to be taken by whom, how and when?

AUDIT REPORTS

There are two types of auditor: the **external auditor** and the **internal auditor**. The role of the former is laid down by statute and in case law; that of the latter, while also affected to some extent by case law, is ultimately what management wants it to be. Therefore the structure of audit reports will depend on the type of audit work being undertaken.

External auditors are independent of the companies on which they report. They are required to report to the shareholders at general meetings on whether the final statements of a company give a 'true and fair view' of the state of the company's affairs. If they are uncertain, or if they do not believe this to be so, they must say so in what is known as a **qualified audit report**. Various Auditing Standards give the wording appropriate to qualified and unqualified reports. It is now normal practice also for external auditors to issue **reports to management** which are more akin to internal audit reports.

Internal auditors are concerned with the segregation of duties and the internal control of the business for which they are employed. The structure of their reports tends to be fairly consistent, but it is *not* defined by any Auditing Standards.

What points should I bear in mind?

In a few words the external auditor commits himself or herself to a high degree of responsibility. If the contents of the report do not reflect the due care, skill and diligence expected of a qualified person, the auditor may be held liable for damages. It is essential, therefore, that the report should be carefully prepared to reflect an opinion within the limits of the examination, and sufficiently clear as to leave no likelihood of misinterpretation by those whom it concerns.

The internal auditor does not face such an onerous responsibility because the report is not written for the same audience – it is for internal consumption (although the external auditor may decide to place some reliance upon it). However, like all report writers, the internal auditor must always strive for objectivity and accuracy.

What would be a suitable format?

As stated above, the wording of qualified and unqualified external audit reports are given in various Auditing Standards, for example

A5 and G3102 (the 'true and fair' report). There are several other standard reports, but they will not be reproduced here.

An external auditor's report to management will include any or all of the following sections:

1. Weaknesses in internal control and recommendations on how they may be rectified.

2. Breakdowns in the accounting systems and any material errors arising.

3. Additional audit time required as a result of either section 1 or 2, or the clients' failure to adhere to timetables.

4. Unsatisfactory accounting procedures or policies, and recommendations as to how they may be improved.

5. Suggestions as to how financial and accounting efficiency may be improved.

6. Constructive suggestions not necessarily related to accounting procedures but noted by the auditor during the course of his or her investigations, with the benefit of an outsider's viewpoint.

A suitable format for an internal audit report is as follows:

1. Contents page

2. Summary (the main findings, conclusions and recommendations)

3. Introduction (what broad subjects were audited, where and when)

4. Scope (what precisely was audited, and possibly what was not)

5. Main body (the findings, divided into logical sub-sections)

6. Conclusions (flowing naturally from the main body)

7. Recommendations (flowing naturally from the conclusions)

8. Appendixes

COMPARATIVE TESTING REPORTS

Perhaps the best known of these reports is *Which* magazine. Its purpose is to select a number of standards, make comparisons of these standards from item to item, and then reach logical conclusions and recommendations about which are the best and/or which represent the best value for money.

What points should I bear in mind?
It is essential to choose *sensible* standards and then to define them very carefully at the beginning of the report. Here are some standards important in any well-designed product:

- Does it work properly? A pop-up toaster should pop up toast.
- Is it fit for its purpose? A portable television should be portable.
- Can it cope with the likely conditions of use? A public telephone should be vandal-resistant.
- Is it durable and easy to maintain for its expected lifespan? For example, are spare parts readily available?
- Is it safe and easy to use? A cooker should have no sharp edges and its controls should be clear.
- Is it pleasing to look at and to handle? Wallpaper must be attractive to potential customers.
- Does it have 'style'? A well-designed product combines a careful choice of colours, patterns and textures. It should be aesthetically pleasing.

Obviously the precise standards you choose will depend on the items being compared. Here are some examples of standards important when choosing a telephone:

- Target price (comparing similar models)
- Colour options
- Features:
    - last number redial
    - number of memories
    - a display
    - battery back-up
    - weight of handset
    - maximum loudness of ring

What would be a suitable format?

There are two basic ways of presenting these reports. The first is to define the first standard and then compare the performance of each item before moving on to the next standard. The second is to name the first item and then record how it matches up to various standards, before moving on to the next item.

There are three customary formats for comparative testing reports, as follows:

Comparison by Standard – Format A
1. Contents page
2. Introduction
3. Explanation and description of items to be compared
4. Comparison by Standard:

Standard A
- Item (i)
- Item (ii)
- Item (iii)

Standard B
- Item (i)
- Item (ii)
- Item (iii)

Etc.

5. Conclusions
6. Recommendations

Comparison by Standard – Format B
1. Contents page
2. Introduction
3. Summary of Standards and Data
4. Conclusions
5. Recommendations
6. Appendixes

    (i)   Explanation and description of items to be compared
    (ii) Comparison by Standard A:
        – Explanation of Standard A
        – Comparison of items

(ii) Comparison by Standard B:
  – Explanation of Standard B
  – Comparison of items
Etc.

Comparison by Items
1. Contents page
2. Introduction
3. Explanation of Standards
4. Comparison by items:

  Item (i):
    – Standard A
    – Standard B
    – Standard C

  Item (ii):
    – Standard A
    – Standard B
    – Standard C

  Etc.

5. Conclusions
6. Recommendations

If the comparison requires quite sophisticated technological investigation, you should also consider the use of formats B or C of **Technological Reports** (see page 146-8).

DUTY NOTES REPORTS

See **Instructional Manuals** (page 131-2)

EXPLANATORY REPORTS

These are *factual* reports which provide an account of something that has happened.

What points should I bear in mind?
You must be unbiased and objective. Do not give any recommendations unless you are asked to do so.

What would be a suitable format?

This is a suitable format for an explanatory report:

1. Contents page
2. Introduction
    - Why was the report prepared, and who requested it?
    - Give a 'pen picture' of whatever has happened.
    - What is the position and authority of the writer?
3. Persons involved
    - Give their names and positions, where relevant.
4. Sequence of events
    - A simple, straightforward account of what happened.
5. Action taken
    - List all the critical actions taken in the order in which they occurred and the reasons for them. If necessary use appendixes.
6. Cause and effect
    - What were the causes and effects of these actions?
7. Conclusions
    - How was the information for the report gathered?
    - How long did this take?
    - What degree of accuracy can the reader reasonably assume?
    - Are any important facts omitted?
    - If so, why?
8. Recommendations
    - If required.
9. Appendixes
    - See section 5.

See also **Informative Reports** (page 130).

FEASIBILITY REPORTS

These discuss the practicality, and possibly the suitability and compatibility of a given project, both in physical and economic terms. They also discuss the desirability of the proposed project from the viewpoint of those who would be affected by it. Report writers must come to a *conclusion*, and must *recommend* that some action is taken or is not taken and/or that some choice is adopted or is rejected.

What points should I bear in mind?

You must be unbiased and your approach must be logical. Be sure that you know the precise **purpose** of the proposed project and also its **scope**. See also **Systems Evaluation Reports** (page 143).

What would be a suitable format?

This is a suitable format for a feasibility report:

1. Abstract
2. Summary
3. Contents list (including a separate list of illustrations)
4. Glossary
5. Introduction (purpose and scope)
6. Discussion (the main body providing the evidence – use appendixes if necessary)
7. Conclusions (flowing naturally from the discussion)
8. Recommendations (flowing naturally from the conclusions)
9. References (if necessary)
10. Appendixes (see section 6)

Sometimes sections 1 and 2 are combined.

INFORMATIVE REPORTS

These are more general than explanatory reports (see above), but there is a degree of overlap. The purpose of an informative report is to increase the readers' knowledge of an event or to bring them up to date.

What points should I bear in mind?

You must present a clear overall theme. Each section of the report must be appropriate to this theme; there must be a good reason for including it. It is important to provide a logical plan because some readers may be interested in perhaps just one or two sections of the report.

What would be a suitable format?

This is a customary format for an informative report:

1. Contents page
2. Introduction (why was the report produced and what is hoped to be achieved by it?)
3. Plan (how the Main Body is structured)
4. Main Body (possibly one subsection for each main piece of information)
5. Conclusions (flowing naturally from the Main Body – also what, if anything, is it hoped will happen next?)

Sometimes sections 2 and 3 are combined. See also **Explanatory Reports** (page 128).

INSTRUCTIONAL MANUALS

Instructional manuals and duty notes are written to explain *how* a job or process (or perhaps how a particular aspect of a job or a process) is to be performed.

What points should I bear in mind?
Good instructional manuals and duty notes are written by people who know the job or process well. They know how much detailed instruction to include, and how much to leave out. Once you have drafted your instructions, try them out first on someone who is likely to use the report.

Do not confuse instructional manuals with **Process Description Reports** (see page 136). As already stated, the former explain *how* a process is to be performed; the latter help the reader *understand* that process. So be absolutely sure of your purpose before deciding on a suitable format.

What would be a suitable format?
This is a typical format for an instructional manual or a set of duty notes:

1. Contents page
2. Job/Duty/Process objective (a brief statement of subject, purpose and scope)
3. Theory or principles of the operation (the mechanics of the process)
4. List of materials and equipment needed
5. Description of the mechanism (an overview of the equipment, possibly breaking it into its component parts – see Chapter 8)
6. List and number of steps necessary to complete the job

7. Instructions for each step (the main body)
8. Precautions necessary (explain why)
9. Show what must be done (use illustrations to support section 7 – see Chapter 8)
10. The degree of difficulty at each stage

Sections 3-5 and 8 are often omitted from clerical duty notes.

INTERVIEW REPORTS

Effective interviewing techniques are not within the scope of this book. However, a brief discussion on the preparation of interview reports is appropriate.

What points should I bear in mind?
Clear and adequate reports are essential to an interviewer who seeks a detailed and accurate recall and evaluation of interviewees (perhaps job applicants). Interviewers who lack the technique of interview report writing will merely attempt to rationalise their decision.

There are two types of interview report. The first is designed to ensure that an interview is well-structured, comprehensive, and that adequate and relevant notes are taken. The second is used to evaluate the material gathered during the interview.

What would be a suitable format?
The following format provides a useful framework for an interview. There will also be several sub-subheadings which are not given here. However the framework must be used with discretion. A good interview is **organic**, not mechanical.

A Structured Interview Report
1. Interviewee, interviewer, reference, date, time and location
2. Physical:
   - First impression
   - Appearance
   - Speech
   - Health
3. Attainments:
   - Work
   - Educational
   - Extramural

4. Interests
5. Circumstances:
    - Family background
    - Domestic and social situation
6. Special aptitudes
7. General intelligence
8. Disposition

After the interview the interviewer will need to evaluate the interviewees. This report format will be of assistance:

An Interview Evaluation Summary Report
1. Interviewee, interviewer, reference, date, time and location
2. Able to do
3. Willing to do:
    - Disposition
    - Motivation
4. Summary
5. Recommendation

Before sections 2 and 3 can be completed the candidate will first be given a raw score of 1-5 (poor to outstanding) for every ability and willingness raised by the interviewer. However, as some of these qualities will be more important to the job than others, they will all be given a weighting, or relative importance score (often 1-7; useful to vital). The raw score will then be multiplied by the weighting, and the separate products will be totalled.

The top scorer is not necessarily the best candidate. For example, there may be a minimum total required for some or all the qualities, and these may not have all been met. However, this method does force the interviewer to think about the specific requirements of the job, and about how far the various interviewees meet them.

INVESTIGATION INTO THE FINANCIAL AFFAIRS OF A COMPANY REPORTS

There are numerous types of investigation – some private (for example, ones undertaken on behalf of a prospective purchaser of a business); others governed by statute (for example, reports for prospectuses and for Department of Trade investigations).

What points should I bear in mind?

In the case of a private investigation, the accountant must obtain precise instructions from his or her client (the terms of reference). In the case of an investigation governed by statute, the reporting accountant must be fully conversant with the statutory regulations, and must also obtain necessary instructions where applicable.

Throughout the investigation never lose sight of your purpose. It is all too easy to become side-tracked. First make preliminary inquiries to ascertain the information that is necessary to be able to plan the investigation. Draft a skeletal framework, detailing the headings which will be used in the final report. Then undertake all the necessary detailed work, recording your findings on working papers. From these the final report will be drafted.

What would be a suitable format?

This will depend on the nature of the investigation, but a typical structure is as follows:

1. Introduction (including the terms of reference and the nature and history of the enterprise being investigated)
2. Main body (the work performed and the facts ascertained – see below)
3. Conclusions (drawn from the main body)
4. Recommendations (drawn from the conclusions)
5. Appendixes (any voluminous statistics)

In the case of an investigation into a retail business on behalf of a potential purchaser, section 2 – the main body – could be subdivided as follows:

- 2.1 Management and Staff

- 2.2 Sales and Marketing

- 2.3 Purchases and Supplies

- 2.4 Trade Results (per audited accounts)

- 2.5 Prospects and Trends

- 2.6 Assets and Liabilities

MINUTES

Minutes can be defined as a written record of the business transacted at a meeting. They may well have some legal and authoritative force.

What points should I bear in mind?

As a general rule, the fewer the words used the better. Ask yourself, what was the **purpose** of the meeting? Minutes of a formal meeting must include: decisions taken, motions passed and the names of the people who attended. Those of a **standing committee** must provide enough information and discussion so that absent members can participate on equal terms at the next meeting. Minutes of a **subcommittee** must include enough to keep its parent committee in touch with developments and to explain the reasons for decisions.

Write in the simple past tense (Mr Smith reported that . . .), and as soon as possible after the meeting. Selective note taking at the meeting will greatly assist this process (see Chapter 2 – Listening and Traditional notes, pages 36 and 44). Concentrate on *conclusions*. Do not record controversy; state what was decided.

The way minutes are numbered varies from organisation to organisation. Here are three common methods:

- consecutively, from the first meeting onwards;

- consecutively, beginning each set of minutes with '1'; and

- consecutively, beginning each year with '1'.

Check that your minutes:

- provide a true, impartial and balanced account of the proceedings;

- are written in clear, concise and unambiguous language;

- are as concise as is compatible with the degree of accuracy required;

- follow a method of presentation which helps the reader assimilate the contents.

Once the minutes have been drafted, ask the chairperson to check them. Then circulate them to everyone who attended the meeting and also to anyone else who will be expected to act upon them. It is a good idea to clearly identify these people by putting their names in an 'action' column on the right of the page and opposite the appropriate references in the text.

If someone asks for a correction, try to negotiate an acceptable form of words. However do not be fooled by people who want you to report what they *should* have said, not what they *actually* said. At the following meeting these minutes will be discussed and any arguments over them will be resolved. The chairperson will then sign them as correct.

What would be a suitable format?

Headings in the minutes of a meeting should broadly correspond with those which appear in its agenda, as follows:

1.   Heading (including where and when the meeting was held)
2.   Present (who was there)
3.   Apologies for Absence (who should have been there, but was not)
4.   Minutes of the Previous Meeting (note any corrections and state 'The minutes were accepted as a true record of the meeting [with the above corrections]')
5. ⎫
6. ⎬ Simple statements of what actually occurred at the meeting
7. ⎬
8. ⎭
9.   Any Other Business (the 'leftovers')
10.   Date of Next Meeting (also give the time and location)

PROCESS DESCRIPTION REPORTS

A process is a specific series of actions that bring about a specific result.

What points should I bear in mind?

It is important not to confuse instructional manuals (see above) with process description reports. The former explain *how* a process is to be performed; the latter help the reader *understand* that process. Process description reports are used to describe the following:

- How something is made

- How something is done (for information, not instruction)

- How a mechanism works

- How a natural process occurs

The report is essentially chronological or sequential and it is most commonly used within the world of business and industry. Almost every such report will include illustrations (see Chapter 8).

What would be a suitable format?
A suitable format for a process description report would be as follows:

1. Contents page (with a separate list of illustrations)
2. Introduction (identify the process; record its purpose and significance; give an overview of the steps involved)
3. Main body (discuss each step in turn)
4. Summary (concentrate on the purpose and importance of the actions or the significance of the facts)

PROGRESS REPORTS

These are **periodic** reports which, as their name suggests, describe how some activity or process is progressing. They are often built up from workers' daily logs, supervisors' reports, and so on.

What points should I bear in mind?
Progress reports will be required in one of three circumstances:

- on a regular basis;

- at certain times during an activity or process; or

- as and when required.

They record progress over a specific period of time, and they make comparisons from period to period by identifying changes and their underlying causes and effects. They are essential for effective decision making so they must be clear, accurate and unambiguous.

What would be a suitable format?

Most organisations have standard printed progress report forms, although headings vary considerably. Here is one simple format:

1. Introduction
    - the period of work covered– the work planned– the authority for the work– the progress to date
2. Main Body
    - the work completed– how the work has been completed
3. Summary
    - the work planned for the future– an overall appraisal of the progress to date

RESEARCH REPORTS

The purpose of a research report is to extend our understanding of the world by reducing uncertainty and increasing our understanding of it.

What points should I bear in mind?

Results alone are never enough. As you will see from the typical format described below, you must be able to assess and then evaluate the *reliability* of the results. You must say precisely how the work was carried out, what methods were used to collect the data, and how it was analysed. Conclusions and recommendations must be drafted with great care.

What would be a suitable format?

This is a typical format for a research report:

1. Contents page
2. Introduction
    - Set the scene; give a clear statement of the objectives and scope of the research.
    - What was known about the subject at the beginning of the research?
    - Put the project into its proper context.
    - Give the reason(s) for the research.
    - Discuss the events which led up to it.
    - Assess the importance of other, related work.

3. Work carried out
   - Describe the overall shape and design of the research.
   - Describe the methods used (for example, sampling methods).
   - Describe the actual work carried out, probably in chronological order.
   - Explain how the results were analysed (for example, input to a computer).
4. The Results
   - In an academic report, give full results (with an interpretation in a separate section).
   - In a non-academic report, you can omit some results (or at least put them in an appendix) and emphasise significant results.
   - Concentrate on each objective of the research in turn.
   - Structure your results around these objectives.
   - Discuss the results; form links; build up an overall picture.
   - Distinguish 'facts' from interpretations, inferences, predictions or deductions.
5. Conclusions
   - Make sure they flow naturally from the results.
   - Each one must be supported by your findings and/or other research.
   - If no clear picture has emerged, then say so.
   - Do not see relationships that do not exist.
6. Recommendations
   - These should flow naturally from your conclusions, with no surprises.
7. Appendixes
   - Include items which would disturb the flow of the report (for example, survey forms and questionnaires).

SCIENTIFIC REPORTS

A scientific report consists of an account of a test or experiment, of its findings, and of its conclusions.

What points should I bear in mind?

Before you can write the report, you must carry out the test or experiment accurately and you must record your results as you proceed. Here are some points to bear in mind:

- Make sure you understand the purpose of the test or experiment.

- If you are not familiar with the relevant theory, look it up before you start.

- Make sure you select appropriate equipment with reference to its accuracy, sensitivity and safety. Ensure you know how the equipment works, and then set it up in the most sensible way for you to make all the required measurements and observations.

- Carry out the test or experiment, recording *every* observation as you proceed. Ensure you observe and record accurately.

- Always record the units of measurement. All readings must be consistent, for example to two decimal places.

- There is no point in giving a reading of, say, 0.2317mm unless you have a good reason to believe that it lies somewhere between 0.231 and 0.232mm. If you do not have good reason to believe this, then record the result only to the degree of precision to which you have confidence – perhaps 0.23mm.

- Record the estimated limits of error. If a spring can measure with an accuracy of plus or minus 0.1mm, you should record this as, say,

    length of spring = 21.7 ± 0.1mm

- If you add a mass to the spring and re-measure, the error could be plus or minus 0.1mm on both figures; so record this as, say,

    change of length of spring = 14.9 ± 0.2mm

- Calculate the results and draw any necessary rough graphs in pencil. If the results are unreasonable or inconsistent (out of line), then make the tests again.

- Form a conclusion based on your accumulated evidence.

- Write the report.

What would be a suitable format?
This is the usual format for a scientific report:

1. Name of class, group or department; experiment number; reference; date and time.
   - The time is relevant only if it is likely to affect results (for example, was barometric pressure a factor?).

2. Title of experiment.

3. Summary (or Abstract or Synopsis)
   - A brief statement about the structure of the report; why the experiment was carried out; what you found, and the significance of what you found.

4. Contents page

5. Introduction
   - Your purpose and scope.

6. Apparatus
   - A list of apparatus and details of its arrangements, with diagrams.

7. Circuit theory
   - Where applicable. A brief account of the theory underlying the experiment.

8. Method
   - A full and clear account of how the experiment was carried out. Write in the passive (A glass stopper was weighed).

9. Results (or Findings)
   - All your readings neatly tabulated with graphs neatly drawn. Give the estimated limits of error (see above). If necessary use appendixes.

10. Conclusion (or Discussion)
    - The inferences drawn from the results obtained (these results show . . .). Interpret results and explain their significance.
    - Could this experiment have been improved in some way? If so, explain why and how.

11. Appendixes
    - To support section 9, if necessary.

STUDENT PROJECT REPORTS

Many students are required to undertake projects and produce reports. For example, they are an important part of many GCSE examination schemes.

What points should I bear in mind?

Here are some points to bear in mind when carrying out a project:

- Be aware of who will choose the topic. It may be chosen by your teacher, or by you, or through discussion between the two of you.
- The topic chosen must be acceptable to your examining group. So talk to your teacher and refer to your syllabus. Then select a **suitable topic**, preferably one that can be investigated locally.
- Decide what sources of information you will require (see Chapters 1 and 2).
- Decide how you will gather this information (see Chapter 2).
- Gather the information (see Chapter 2).
- Analyse the information (see Chapter 2).
- Write the report (see Chapter 3).

If you want to know more about student project reports, refer to Chapters 9 and 10 of *How to Succeed at GCSE*, John Bowden, Cassell, 1989.

What would be a suitable format?

If your teacher tells you the required format, or if it is given in your syllabus, comply with it. If you have no such instruction or guidance, consider this simple format:

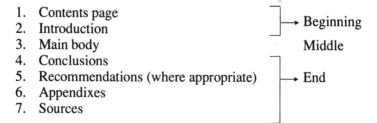

1. Contents page
2. Introduction   → Beginning
3. Main body   Middle
4. Conclusions
5. Recommendations (where appropriate)   → End
6. Appendixes
7. Sources

See also **Technological Reports** (page 145).

SYSTEMS EVALUATION REPORTS

A systems evaluation report serves one of these purposes:

- To discover which system out of several alternatives is most suitable for a particular application.

- To test an apparatus or system which it is intended to employ on a large scale, or with multiple applications, if the initial operation is deemed worthwhile.

- To enquire into the causes of failures in an existing operational system.

The last of these is considered under **Trouble-Shooting Reports** (page 148).

What points should I bear in mind?

The purpose of the first two types of report is to inform those concerned with selection, implementation and utilisation about:

- the requirements of the application;

- the criteria by which the systems should be judged;

- the features of available systems;

- data on their performance in the field; and

- recommendations or conclusions about the best course of action.

These reports are important – mistakes are costly. You must be independent; do not rely on the word of manufacturers or suppliers. You probably will need to use supplementary text, footnotes, a glossary and illustrations (diagrams, flow charts and perhaps photographs).

What would be a suitable format?

A suitable format for a report with the purpose of discovering which system out of several alternatives is most suitable for a particular application is as follows:

1. Contents page
2. Preface (personal background: why have *you* written the report?)
3. System Requirements
4. Systems Available
5. Criteria for Selection
6. The Final Choice
7. Appendixes (System Data Sheets).

A report on the initial performance of an apparatus or a system could follow this format:

1. Contents page
2. Preface (personal background: why have *you* written the report?)
3. Apparatus/System Requirements
4. Apparatus/System Performance (use appendixes, if necessary)
5. Conclusions
6. Recommendation
7. Appendixes (to support section 4, if necessary).

See also **Feasibility Reports** (page 129) and **Trouble-Shooting Reports** (page 148).

TECHNICAL REPORTS

Technical reports are often written at an early stage in a production process. They are usually generated internally, either by the technical publications department of an organisation or by staff involved in this production process. Here are some examples of technical reports:

- a technical proposal

- a feasibility study

- design and research reports

- pre-production reports

- evaluation documents

- ad hoc reports

What points should I bear in mind?

These reports are often written by engineers who are not always familiar with the techniques of effective writing. The advice given throughout this book, therefore, will be of assistance. If you wish to read more about this wide yet specialised area of report writing, refer to *A Beginner's Guide to Technical Writing*, John Evans, Newnes Technical Books, 1983.

What would be a suitable format?

Every organisation will have its own format requirements. This is a typical layout:

1. Contents page
2. Aims (why it was written, its terms of reference and its general purpose)
3. Summary (the salient facts and a concise summary of conclusions, if any)
4. Main body (main discussion of the subject matter)
5. Conclusions (if necessary)
6. Bibliography (if required)
7. Index (in larger reports only)

TECHNOLOGICAL REPORTS

A technological report is concerned with the application of practical or mechanical sciences in order to achieve a desired aim.

What points should I bear in mind?

A good technological report should combine and *demonstrate* these qualities:

- planning

- communication

- ability to reason

- ability to evaluate

- a logical and realistic solution

Show the 'thinking' that has gone into the report. Make sure it is well organised and well-presented. Present it logically to show a well-constructed development of the problem-solving process. Reach a solution which achieves your objective. Evaluate your work: are you satisfied with it? Is it economically viable?

What would be a suitable format?

Here are three formats. As always, select the one that best suits your needs:

Format A
1. Contents page
2. Brief (what you were attempting to do)
3. Analysis (your analysis of the problem – include the research material you have gathered)
4. Thinking (your initial thinking and your evaluation of it)
5. Solution (explain how you developed your solution)
6. Evidence (include drawings, photographs and other evidence of your solution – the artefact)
7. Evaluation (an objective evaluation of your solution)

This format would be suitable for a **Student Project Report** about the production of an artefact (a physical thing created by one or more human beings, such as a working model or a piece of wood-work).

Format B
1. Contents page
2. Purpose
   - why was the work undertaken?
3. Methods Used
   - the apparatus and equipment used (with illustrations)
   - a step-by-step account of the procedure
   - observations taken (tabulated) – use appendixes, if necessary
   - calculations necessary to give meaning to the observations
4. Results
   - use tables and illustrations (and appendixes, if necessary)

5. Conclusions
   - a survey of the work undertaken:
     - compare actual results with theoretical results
     - compare actual results with others obtained elsewhere
     - give reasons for such discrepancies or variations
     - assess the relevance of the methods used
     - assess the efficiency of the equipment used
     - discuss any human errors and/or any relevant environmental factors
6. Recommendations
   - flowing naturally from your conclusions
7. Appendixes
   - to support sections 3 and/or 4, if necessary

Format C
1. Contents page
2. Summary
   - concentrate on your findings
3. Object
   - a brief statement of your aim
4. Introduction
   - why was the work undertaken?
   - provide any relevant background information
   - discuss any limitations/conditions you faced (for example: cost, time, or environmental)
5. Apparatus
   - describe it (with illustrations)
   - why was it chosen?
6. Procedures
   - a step-by-step account of what was done
7. Observations
   - give details of components, specimens, equipment or machinery during and after the test
   - record the readings made during the investigation in tables and/or illustrations – use appendixes, if necessary
8. Calculations
   - based on your observations
   - based on theoretical considerations
   - analyse errors
   - summarise your results

9. Results
   - use a separate section or appendix, if necessary
10. Comments
    - discuss the degree of accuracy achieved
    - compare your results with those from other sources
    - comment on quality of the materials and workmanship of the item tested
    - what alternative method(s) of presenting your findings could you have used?
    - why did you present your findings as you have?
    - make your acknowledgements
11. Conclusions
    - flowing from your results and, where appropriate, your comments
12. Recommendations
    - flowing from your conclusions
13. Appendixes
    - to support sections 7 and/or 9, if necessary
14. Index
    - in larger reports only

Formats B and C are suitable for technological tests or investigations, perhaps assessing the suitability of two or more items for a defined purpose. Format C is particularly useful for a long report. See also **Comparative Testing Reports** (page 126-8).

TROUBLE-SHOOTING REPORTS

These reports aim to locate the cause of some problem, and then suggest ways to remove or treat it. In the main they deal with people, organisations or hardware.

What points should I bear in mind?
These reports highlight problems. When they are caused by people you must be especially careful to word the report thoughtfully. Be candid but be fair. Most of all, be accurate. When you are discussing problems caused by the structure of an organisation, you must expect to meet the objection: 'But we've always done it this way'. People are generally not keen on change. Reports on hardware are less complicated and often less contentious.

What would be a suitable format?

Here are four possible structures. Choose the one that best suits your needs:

Format A
1. Contents page

2. Present situation (the salient points)

3. Options for Change (the pros and cons of each option)

4. Recommendations (well-argued, clear, unambiguous and concise)

5. References (if required)

Format B
1. Contents page

2. Introduction (purpose and scope)

3. Evidence (concise, balanced and unambiguous – use appendixes, if necessary)

4. Arguments for (present all the pros logically and objectively and respond positively to weaknesses in your case)

5. Arguments against (list them and refute them in turn)

6. Recommendation (be clear, unambiguous and precise)

7. Appendixes (to support section 3, if necessary)

Format C
1. Contents page

2. Introduction (your purpose)

3. Summary of Recommendations (clear, unambiguous and precise)

4. Present Position (the salient points)

5. Scope (what work was done, and possibly what was not)

6. Observations on Recommendations (the main body – repeat each recommendation and give the main pros and cons for each – say why the pros prevailed)

7. Conclusion (keep it brief)

8. Appendixes (if required)

Format D

1. Contents page

2. The Problem
    - nature and cause
    - extent
    - effects (perhaps on safety or production)

3. The Need for Change
    - reasons (perhaps labour problems or competition)

4. Proposed Solution
    - options available
    - details of proposed solution
    - previous experience of this scheme (perhaps elsewhere)
    - advantages
    - disadvantages (and how they can be overcome)
    - effects (perhaps improved efficiency or sales prospects)

5. Time Factors
    - when can it be implemented?

6. Costs
    - for *each* option:
    - implementation costs
    - running costs
    - estimated savings, if applicable

7. Conclusion
    - for the *chosen* option:
    - overall effects
    - overall benefits

8. Recommendations
    - item by item, clear and unambiguous

9. Appendixes
    - if required

See also **Feasibility Reports** (page 129) and **Systems Evaluation Report** (page 143).

Report Writing: A Checklist

Finally, here is a report writing checklist:

PREPARATION AND PLANNING

1. Do you have clear, unambiguous terms of reference?
2. Are you sure about the precise purpose of the report?
3. Have you defined your overall objective(s)?
4. Have you identified and assessed your readers?
5. Do you know what resources are at your disposal?
6. Have you identified the information you will need?
7. Have you drawn up a suitable skeletal framework?

COLLECTING AND HANDLING INFORMATION

8. Have you established where the information can be found?
9. Have you used the most appropriate method(s) to collect this information?
10. Have you recorded your findings in a sensible and logical manner?
11. Are you satisfied that the information is accurate, objective and complete?
12. Is your evidence strong?
13. Have you amended your skeletal framework, if necessary, so that your findings will make an impact on your readers?
14. Have you sorted and grouped the information sensibly, based on your (amended) skeletal framework?
15. Do you have enough relevant information to cover each section and subsection of the planned report?

WRITING THE REPORT

16. Does your title page include:
    - concise title (and subtitle) which clearly identifies the report;
    - the name (and designation) and the writer(s);
    - the date the report was issued;

       – copyright information, if required; and
       – the distribution list?

17. Have you written the main body and appendixes first?

18. Have you checked the main body and appendixes to ensure that:
    – facts and arguments are presented in a logical, sectional or creative sequence, as required;
    – the overall structure and layout are appropriate;
    – the tone and balance are correct;
    – tables and illustrations are appropriate and well-presented;
    – figures and calculations are accurate; and
    – spelling and punctuation are correct?

19. Have you then written your conclusions, recommendations, introduction, summary and any other necessary report components?

20. Are your conclusions:
    – warranted, given the facts presented in the main body and appendixes;
    – clearly, simply and objectively stated, and not exaggerated; and
    – written with the likely impact on the readers clearly in mind?

21. Are your recommendations:
    – warranted, given your conclusions
    – specific, stating who should do what, when, and how; and
    – written with the likely impact on the readers clearly in mind?

22. Does your introduction set the scene and include everything your readers will need to know before they read the rest of the report?

23. Does your summary stimulate the readers' interest by outlining the salient points and the main conclusions and recommendations?

24. Have you used simple methods of numbering and headings, and are all numbers and headings on your contents page identical to those which appear in the text?

25. Have you, a colleague and your line manager checked the entire draft?

26. Have you amended the draft as necessary before sending it to the typist or printer?

27. Have you proof-checked the report in detail?

28. Has your line manager approved the final version of the report?

29. Have sufficient copies been made, and have they been properly bound?

30. Have all copies of the report (and covering letters or compliment slips) been issued at the same time, and have these issues been recorded in a register?

Further Reading

A good dictionary is an essential tool for any writer expecting his or her work to be read by others. Chambers, Collins, Longman and Oxford University Press each offers a comprehensive range to suit every need and every pocket.

The Complete Plain Words, 2nd edition, Sir Ernest Gowers (Penguin 1987). An excellent guide to using plain English and avoiding jargon.

Copyediting: The Cambridge Handbook, 2nd edition, Judith Butcher (Cambridge University Press 1981). An authoritative text used by professional publishers and their editors.

Dictionary of Modern English Usage, 2nd edition, H.W. Fowler, revised by Sir Ernest Gowers (Oxford University Press 1965). A classic guide to English usage, full of fascinating information.

How to Master Business English, Michael Bennie (How To Books 1991). A very practical, straightforward and comprehensive book illustrated with numerous examples.

How to Publish A Newsletter, Graham Jones (How To Books 1992). A complete step-by-step handbook which covers all the basics from editing right through to publication.

How to Write for Publication, Chriss McCallum (How To Books 1989). A really writer-friendly introduction for everyone wishing to write articles, books, dramatic or other works.

How to Write and Speak Better (Readers Digest Association Ltd. 1991). Excellent but expensive.

Learn to Draw Charts and Diagrams Step-by-Step, Bruce Robertson (Macdonald Orbis 1988). It starts with basic pie charts and ends with sophisticated computer graphic programs.

Mind the Stop, G.V. Carey (Penguin 1971). Everything you ever wanted to know about punctuation.

The Oxford Dictionary for Writers and Editors (Oxford University Press 1981).

The Oxford Writers' Dictionary, compiled by R.E. Allen (Oxford University Press 1990).

Roget's Thesaurus. You cannot find a word you have forgotten or do not know in a dictionary. Look up a word of similar meaning in Roget and you will find a variety of words and expressions which should include the one in the back of your mind, or perhaps an unfamiliar word which, when checked in a dictionary, proves even more appropriate. There are many versions available, including a revision by E.M. Kirkpatrick (Longman 1987).

Titles and Forms of Address – A Guide to Their Correct Use, 19th edition (A. & C. Black 1990).

Glossary

Abstract (or **Summary**, or **Synopsis**). A condensed version of a report which outlines the salient points and emphasises the main conclusions and, where appropriate, the main recommendations. It has two functions: either to provide a précis of what the recipient is about to read, or has just read; or to provide a summary of a report if the recipient is not going to read all of it.

Acknowledgements. An author's statement of thanks to people and organisations who helped during the preparation of a report.

Addendum (*pl.* **Addenda**). Additional material; an update or afterthought often produced and circulated after a report has been issued.

Agenda. A type of report listing items to be discussed during a meeting. Therefore it must be drawn up in advance.

Aims. A statement of why a report was written; who requested it, when it was requested; and its terms of reference. It usually appears in the introduction.

Algorithm. A flowchart which will answer a question, or solve a problem, or undertake a procedure within a finite number of steps.

Annual Report. A type of report which lists the achievements and failures of an organisation; a progress report in which every department is accounted for.

Appendix (*pl.* **Appendixes** or **Appendices**). A section of a report which gives details of matters discussed more broadly in the main body. It provides additional information for readers who require it without breaking the thread of argument in the main body for readers who do not.

Appraisal report. A type of report which evaluates a person's performance in his or her current job; identifies methods of improving this performance; and often assesses suitability for another job, promotion and/or a change in salary.

Audit report. An external audit report is addressed to shareholders and contains an independent assessment of whether a company's final statements provide a true and fair view of its affairs. An internal audit report is addressed to the management of a company for which the auditor is employed, and is more concerned with segregation of duties and internal control.

Bar chart. A method of presenting figures visually. Very useful for illustrating relationships between items.

Bias. Errors that occur in statistical sampling if the sample is not random or if the questioning is not objective and consistent. See **Leading question**.

Bibliography. A full list of books and other material used in the preparation of a report. Unlike a reference section, it may also include publications not referred to in the report, but considered potentially valuable or of interest to readers.

Binding. The process of assembling the pages of a report in order and then enclosing them within covers.

Bulleting. A method of highlighting important text by indenting it and placing a bold dot or bullet in front of the first word.

Caption (or **Legend**, or **Underline**). Descriptive words or lines accompanying an illustration.

Centring text. A method of refining the appearance of text where each line is placed centrally between the right and left margins. This can be used for whole blocks of text but is more frequently applied to headings.

Circulation list. See **Distribution list.**

Comparative testing report. A type of report which tests similar items, assessing each against a number of well-defined standards, and reaching logical conclusions and recommendations about which are the best and/or which represent the best value for money. The Consumers' Association *Which* magazine contains such reports.

Components. The various sections which collectively make up a report.

Conclusions. A section of a report where the author links the terms of reference with the findings, as presented in the main body, and reaches clear, simply stated and objective conclusions that are fully supported by evidence and arguments and which come within and satisfy the terms of reference.

Confidentiality. The degree to which the availability of a report is restricted. Reports are often classified as confidential when they contain politically or industrially sensitive information or comment, or when they discuss personnel. Confidential reports should be stamped as such on the title page and should be kept under physically secure conditions.

Contact point. The name, address and telephone number of a person the reader can contact if further enquiry or comment is required. It should be given in a report's covering letter.

Contents page. A list of the various sections of a report in the order in which they appear, with the appropriate page and/or paragraph numbers alongside them. If there are more than just one or two illustrations they should be listed separately below the main contents, giving their captions, figure numbers and page and/or paragraph numbers.

Copyright. Legal protection against the use of literary or artistic property without permission. The protection afforded by English law lasts for the duration of the author's life and fifty years thereafter. Copyright is different from a patent in that it cannot exist in an idea, but only in its expression.

Covering letter. An explanatory letter accompanying a report and including a contact point.

Creative substructure. A substructure where information is presented in an apparently haphazard way. A hybrid of the logical substructure and the sectional substructure.

Cross-reference. A method of directing readers to another part of a report for related information.

Cut-away drawing. A pictorial method of illustrating what something looks like. An object is shown with part or all of its outer casing cut away to reveal its internal components.

Distribution list (or **Circulation list**). A list of people who will see a report; its readership. It usually appears on the title page.

Double spacing. Double the usual space between each line of text. It helps a typist or printer read a manuscript (hand written) report; it makes it easier to correct and amend drafts; and it can help readers of a report. Other line spacings include 0,1/2, 11/2, 21/2 and 3. Obviously the choice will affect the number of lines on a page.

Double striking. A method of emphasising text where the printer overprints the text twice, thereby making the word, phrase, sentence, etc. bold.

Draft. An early version of a report drawn up for initial consideration.

Duty notes report. A type of report which explains how a job is to be performed.

End matter. The pages of a report after the main body – cf **Prelims.**

Explanatory report. A type of report which provides a factual account of something that has happened. More specific than an informative report.

Exploded drawing. A pictorial method of illustrating what something looks like. The components of an object are shown in assembly as if they were spread out along an invisible axis.

Feasibility report. A type of report which discusses the practicality, and possibly the suitability and compatibility of a given project, both in physical and economic terms. It must come to a conclusion and must recommend that some action is taken or is not taken and/or that some choice is adopted or is rejected.

Flowchart. A diagrammatic representation of the sequence of operations in a natural, industrial or organisational system.

Footnote. A note or reference placed at the foot of the relevant page; at the end of the relevant section; or towards the end of a report.

Foreword. An introductory section of a report, similar to a preface and an introduction, but usually written by someone other than the author of the report.

Format. The general appearance of a report including type style, paper, binding, covers, layout, shape and size.

Front matter. See **Prelims.**

Glossary (of Terms) (or **Gloss**). An alphabetical list of unfamiliar difficult, specialised or technical words and phrases, acronyms and abbreviations used in a report.

Gluing. A method of binding a report where the sheets are glued and fixed into the spine of a fabric, card or plastic cover.

Go live. To actually undertake a statistical survey (or to operate a system), as distinct from pilot testing it.

Graph. A method of presenting figures visually. Particularly useful for illustrating detailed relationships between items or to show a trend over time.

Graphics. A general term for the use and the presentation of data in a graphical form, eg bar charts.

Heading. A means of identifying and labelling a block of type. It should be specific; comparatively short; expected, or at least easily interpreted; and should cover all the ground collectively. It should be more prominent than a subheading, but less prominent than the title. Headings of similar rank should introduce topics of roughly equal importance.

Highlighting. Drawing attention to important parts of the text by methods other than headings eg using upper case or changing spacing.

House-style. A consistent style of report writing developed by and used within an organisation.

Illustration. A pictorial representation of information as distinct from text. Every illustration should have a caption and figure number and must be referred to in the text. If there are more than just one or two illustrations, they should be listed separately on the contents page.

Indentation. A method of refining the appearance of text where the beginning of a line is inset a number of spaces to indicate a new paragraph; for emphasis; or to break up a large passage.

Index. An alphabetical list of items discussed in a report together with their page and/or paragraph numbers. An index should contain more entries than a contents page. Necessary only in a large report.

Indexing. A method of improving the presentation of a report and a way of helping readers find their way around it. The various sections or subsections are separated and distinguished, perhaps by means of overlapping pages or protruding self-adhesive labels.

Informative report. A type of report which increases the readers' knowledge of an event or brings them up to date. More general than an explanatory report.

Instructional manual. A type of report which explains how a process (a specific series of actions that bring about a specific result) is to be performed – of **Process description report.**

Interview report. A type of report which forms the framework of an interview (although it must not dictate it), and which records facts and opinions about a candidate in a consistent format to facilitate subsequent evaluation and comparison with other candidates.

Introduction. A section of a report which sets the scene. It states the author's intentions – the terms of reference – and gives the aims and scope of the report. An introduction must include everything the readers will need to know before they read the rest of the report.

Investigation into the financial affairs of a company report. A type of report concerned with some specific aspect of a company's financial affairs as defined by the terms of reference and/or by statutory regulations.

Isometric drawing. A pictorial method of illustrating what something looks like. Easy to draw but the lack of perspective makes the object look peculiar.

Justification. A method of refining the appearance of text where both the left and the right-hand edges are straight.

KISS. Stands for Keep It Short and Simple. A very useful principle in all aspects and in all stages of report writing.

Layout. The arrangement of illustrations and text.

Leading question. A question phrased as to suggest the answer expected. In statistical sampling it leads to a bias in the results obtained. Therefore it must avoided.

Legend. See **Caption.**

Libel. A false statement of a defamatory nature about another person that tends to damage his or her reputation and which is presented in a permanent form, such as in writing.

Logical substructure. A substructure where procedures or events are discussed in the *sequence* in which they occur or occurred.

Lower case. Non-capital letters – cf **Upper case.**

Main body. The section of a report which contains the main discussion on the subject-matter as defined by the terms of reference.

Minutes. A type of report which provides a record of business transacted at a meeting. It may well have some legal and authoritative force.

Numbering system. A method of identifying the various components of a report for reference and indexing purposes. Keep it simple.

Organisational chart. A diagram which depicts the hierarchy of, and the lines of command within, an organisation.

Orthographic drawing. A pictorial method of illustrating something. It shows the back, front and side elevations of an object. Of little use where the reader needs to know what it actually looks like.

Pareto principle. 80% of what is important is represented by 20% of what exists. Not to be taken literally, but a very useful general concept to consider during all stages of report writing.

Patterned notes. A method of note taking based on the formation of visual links between facts and ideas, both already known and to be discovered. A very useful way of planning a report, as distinct from writing it – cf **Traditional notes.**

Perspective drawing. A pictorial method of illustrating what something looks like. It shows what an object actually looks like. Often difficult to draw.

Pictogram. A method of presenting figures visually by the use of symbols. Very useful for illustrating relationships between items.

Pie chart. A method of presenting figures visually. Very useful for illustrating relative proportions – or how the total pie is divided up.

Pilot test. An initial test of a questionnaire or other statistical device among a small number of respondents (or an initial test of a new system) to highlight any obvious errors, omissions, ambiguities or other shortcomings before it goes live.

Plastic gripper. A method of binding a report by placing a plastic slide grip along the left hand edge of the assembled covers and sheets.

Population. The total number of people or items within a defined group.

Preface. An introductory section to a report. Often used to convey some *personal* background details behind the production of a report.

Prelims (or **Preliminaries**, or **Front matter**). The pages of a report before the main body – cf **End matter**.

Probability theory. A statistical concept concerned with the effects of chance on an event, experiment, or observation. The basis of statistical sampling.

Process description report. A type of report which helps readers understand a process (a specific series of actions that bring about a specific result) – cf **Instructional manual.**

Progress report. A type of report which describes how some activity or process is advancing.

Proof-reading. Checking and making corrections on a document prepared by a typist or printer. It is very important to identify and correct spelling mistakes and errors and inconsistencies in layout before a report is reproduced and issued.

Questionnaire. A method of gathering information by questioning respondents.

Quota sampling. A method of statistical sampling used to obtain a *balanced* view from people based on their sex, age and possibly social class. However, *within* every defined group or population (eg Females, aged 21-30; or Males, aged 41-50), the sample is random.

Random sample. In statistical sampling, each member of the population has an equal chance of being selected.

Readership. The people who will read a report, as listed on the distribution list. The report is written for them so they must be given the information they need and in a form that they can understand without undue effort.

Recommendations. A section of a report where the author states what specific actions should be taken, and by whom and why, given the terms of reference; the findings as presented in the main body; and the conclusions reached. Recommendations therefore must look to the future and should always be realistic. Do not make them unless they are required by the terms of reference.

Reference number. A unique number allocated to a report. It should appear on the title page.

References. A section of a report which provides full details of publications mentioned in the text, or from which extracts have been quoted – cf **Bibliography.**

Report. A document produced to convey information to a specific audience at a certain moment in time.

Research report. A type of report which extends our understanding of the world by reducing our uncertainty and increasing our comprehension of it.

Respondent. A person who answers questions, perhaps posed in the form of a questionnaire.

Ring binding. A method of binding a report where a special machine perforates the binding edge and then threads the binding through the holes in the covers and the report. Looks very professional.

Saddle stitching. A method of binding a report by means of thread or wire through the fold. See **Stitching.**

Sampling. See **Statistical sampling.**

Scientific report. A type of report which gives an account of a test or experiment together with findings and conclusions.

Scope. A statement of what was done, and perhaps what was not done – and why it was not done – if the readers could reasonably have assumed that it would have been. It may also include discussion on the resources available to and utilized by the report writer; the sources of information; the working methods employed; and the structure of the report. It usually appears in the introduction.

Sectional substructure. A substructure where information is presented in meaningful sections, eg the work of each department in turn or each engineering or clerical function in turn.

Simple random sampling. A method of statistical sampling where every person or item in a population has an equal chance of being selected, eg take ten names out of a hat.

Skeletal framework. An initial overall plan of the structure of a report. A well-planned skeletal framework is the key to effective report writing. It may be revised at any stage(s) during the preparation of the report.

Source (of information). Any person, book, organisation etc supplying information or evidence (especially of an original or primary character) used in a report.

Spacing. See **Double spacing.**

SQ3R. A method of reading. Stands for Survey, Question, Read, Recall, Review. The way you read should vary according to the complexity of the material and the reasons for reading it.

Statistical sampling. A method of drawing conclusions about a population by testing a representative sample of it. It is based on probability theory. See **Quota sampling**; **Simple random sampling**; and **Systematic random sampling**

Stitching. A method of binding a report where sheets are folded in the middle to make two single-sided or four double-sided pages, and are then bound by saddle stitching.

Structure. The arrangement of the components which collectively make up a report.

Subheading. A means of more specifically and precisely identifying and labelling a block of type which comes under an overall heading. Do not use too many subheadings; if necessary re-structure the report to have more headings. Make the subheadings less prominent.

Substructure. The arrangement of material within each of the components of a report, although often applied specifically to the main body. See **Logical substructure**; **Sectional substructure**; and **Creative substructure**.

Subtitle. A secondary title expanding the main title.

Summary. See **Abstract**.

Synopsis. See **Abstract**.

Systems evaluation report. A type of report that evaluates which system out of several alternatives is most suitable for a particular application; or which tests an apparatus or system with a view to possible large scale employment or multiple applications; or which enquires into the causes of failures in an existing operational system. When it serves the last of these purposes, it is sometimes referred to as a trouble-shooting report.

Systematic diagram. A visual method of illustrating how items within a system are *connected* to one another, eg the map of the London Underground shows how stations are connected.

Systematic random sampling. A method of statistical sampling where every person or item in a population has an equal chance of being selected, but the choice is made to a prearranged plan, eg every 100th name on the electoral register.

Tally sheet. A sheet used to mark or set down, and later to total, the number of observations of specified items; or to mark or set down, and later to total, the various answers given by all respondents to a questionnaire.

Technical report. A type of report often written at an early stage in a production process.

Technological report. A type of report which is concerned with the application of practical or mechanical sciences in order to achieve a desired aim.

Terms of Reference (T of R). A concise statement of precisely what a report is about. It is essential that these are known/agreed before any work is undertaken and they should be referred to in the introduction.

Text. The words of a report as distinct from its illustrations.

Title. The overall heading of a report; a restatement of the terms of reference, but usually using different words. It should be clear, concise, relevant and unique and should be more prominent than any other heading which appears in the report.

Title page. A sheet at the beginning of a report which bears the main title (and subtitle, where appropriate); the reference number; the name of the author; and other important information. Every report should have a title page.

Traditional notes. A method of note taking where relevant material is condensed using headings and subheadings, with the most important points and arguments being highlighted. This method is also the basis of report writing, as distinct from report planning – cf **Patterned notes**.

Treasury tag. A simple method of binding a report. Holes are made in the pages and covers using a punch and then tags are inserted. Useful where amendments and/or inserts such as maps and plans are expected.

Trouble-shooting report. A type of report which locates the cause of some problem, and then suggests ways to remove or treat it. It can deal with people or organisations; or hardware or systems, where it is sometimes referred to as a systems evaluation report.

Underline. See **Caption**.

Upper case. Capital letters – cf **Lower case**.

Working papers. Notes recording the detailed information, evidence, findings and sources that will form the basis of the main body, and of any appendices. Therefore they must be complete and accurate.

Index